50¢

A Pictorial History of Downhill Skiing

This picture appeared in the ILLUSTRATED PRESS of 1874 and is the world's first illustration of a ski race. The race was one of many held in California's Sierra Nevada Mountains by 19th-century gold miners who battled each other head-to-head, skiing straight down, and who could achieve speeds of over 80 miles per hour on their long "snowshoes." Waxing, or "doping," was a very important factor. The "dopeman" can be seen in the lower right, along with the ever-present outdoor bar. It was reported that "next to drinking, fighting and gambling, snowshoe racing became the principal pastime" in the snowbound mining camps.

WASM

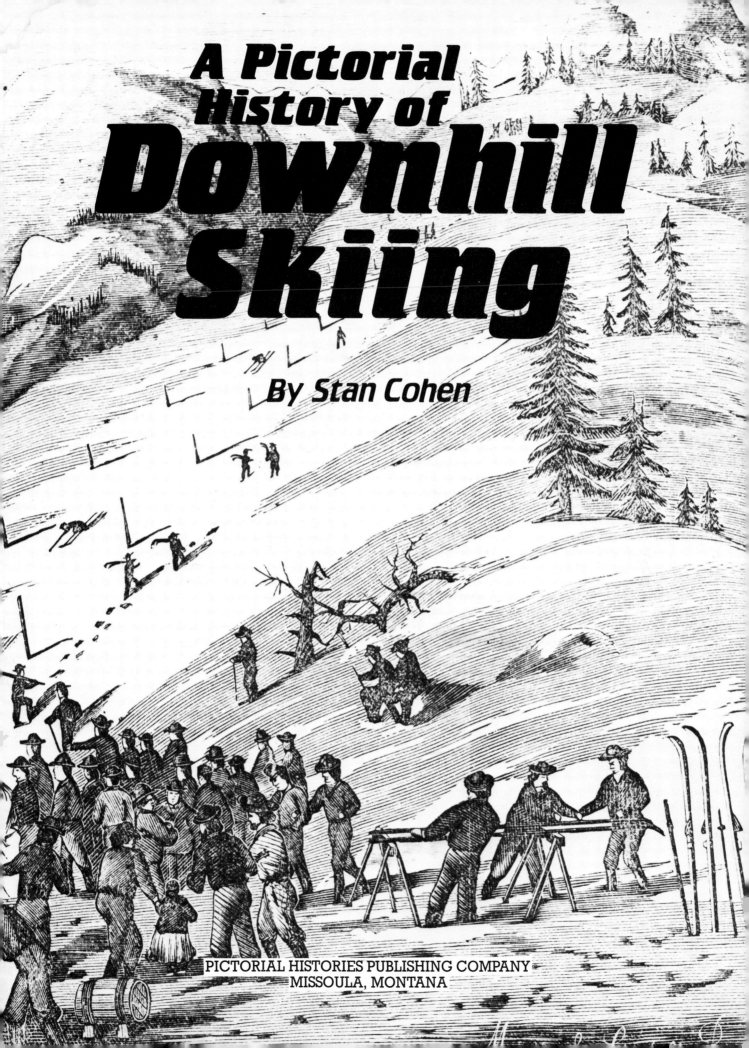

A Pictorial History of Downhill Skiing

By Stan Cohen

PICTORIAL HISTORIES PUBLISHING COMPANY
MISSOULA, MONTANA

LIBRARY OF CONGRESS
CATALOG CARD NUMBER 84-62203

ISBN 9-933126-55-7

First Printing January 1985

PRINTED IN U.S.A.

Typography: Arrow Graphics & Typography
Layout: Stan Cohen
Front Cover Art: Mary Beth Percival, Missoula, Montana
Back Cover: Courtesy Chicago Historical Society

PICTORIAL HISTORIES PUBLISHING COMPANY
713 South Third West
Missoula, Montana

TABLE OF CONTENTS

INTRODUCTION

Previous to the fall of 1963, I had skied only twice in my life—a kid growing up in West Virginia in the 1940s and 50s did not have much opportunity in the way of winter sports. That fall, however, I bumped into a friend, Gerald Askevold, on the main street of Missoula, Mont., the town where I was living at the time. Gerald had just returned from France, and was taking over from his sister as head of the ski school at the local ski area, Missoula Snow Bowl. He asked if I would like to go into partnership with him.

That chance meeting led to 11 years spent in the ski business. I started out as operator of the Snow Bowl's ski shop, plunging in as if I knew what I was doing, literally learning the business from the ground up. Later, when I had learned more, I served as the ski area's co-manager and on its board of directors.

The early 1960s was a transition period in the ski business, especially in the area of equipment development. I was able to experience at close hand the rapid replacement of lace boots by buckles, leather boots by plastic, and wooden skis by metal and fiberglass. At the same time, there was a nationwide boom in ski area development.

When I finally left the ski business in 1974, the industry was hardly recognizable as the one I entered back in 1963. Yet those years were a wonderful part of my life; I still sometimes regret the decision to change careers.

My other main interest has always been the study of history. After a brief career as a museum director in Missoula, I launched into the history-book publishing business in 1976. Eight years and 45 books later, I wondered if I could combine my avid interest in history with my love for skiing. This book is the result.

This is the first attempt in two decades to put together a comprehensive pictorial history on American downhill skiing. John Jay's book, *Ski Down the Years* (1966), has been the "bible" of ski history these many years. Since its publication, of course, the ski world has undergone many changes.

With a subject as broad as the history of skiing, I've had to limit the scope of this book to downhill skiing only, and only as it is practiced in the United States. Certainly skiing has had a long and colorful history in Canada and Europe, and each deserves its own historical endeavors. Likewise, the subjects that are covered in single chapters in this book could be expanded into entire books of their own, and several already have.

My main emphasis here has been photographs. This is a *pictorial* history, and it took me to archives throughout the United States. In selecting photos, I have looked for those that were historically significant as well as those that represented many geographical areas. This at times meant I passed over dramatic, but historically insignificant, "action shots." Along with the photos, I have included a fairly short text that covers the history of skiing in this country. It is intended to be both concise and comprehensive.

Downhill skiing in the U.S. dates back to the California goldfields of the 1850s, a fact that is probably unknown to most of today's skiers. As a sport, downhill skiing essentially dropped from sight for the first two or three decades of this century, while jumping and cross-country skiing took its place. Not until 1936 was downhill skiing introduced to the Winter Olympics.

The 1930s and 1940s was a time of rapid expansion in all aspects of downhill skiing. Along with the Sierra skiing of the 1800s, these decades receive particular attention in this book. Further chapters deal with the history of equipment, clothing, technique and instruction, transportation, racing, and other facets of the sport.

The history of skiing is a fascinating subject that can hardly be covered in detail in one volume. A bibliography at the end of the book provides a list of other works for the reader who wishes to know more. I hope my attempt at bringing ski history to life will encourage readers to explore the topic further.

I also hope that the reader will open this book while relaxing around the fire after a hard day of (lift-serviced) skiing. Only then will he or she truly appreciate the enormous strides the sport has made over the last 100 years. —*Stan Cohen*

ACKNOWLEDGMENTS

This book is the culmination of over three years research conducted throughout the United States. It would not have been possible without the cooperation of many individuals.

Peter Stark edited the entire book and wrote several of its chapters. Peter has been skiing for 25 years, and raced for the Dartmouth ski team in the early 1970s. He holds a master's degree in journalism from the University of Wisconsin, and currently is a freelance writer and editor in Missoula, where he still races on the veteran's circuit.

Without the help of Robert "Bob" Baumrucker of San Francisco this book would not have been completed. Also a product of Dartmouth, Bob prodded me to undertake this project and opened up many doors when I was engaged in research and searching for photos. You will meet him again in the chapter on competition.

The nation's four ski museums were very helpful with both research and photos. I especially want to thank Bill Clark of the Western American SkiSport Museum at Boreal Ridge, Calif.; Ken Luostari of the National Ski Hall of Fame and Museum at Ishpeming, Mich.; Arthur "Dick" March Jr. of the New England Ski Museum, Cannon Mountain, N.H.; and Michelle Cahill of the Colorado Ski Museum at Vail, Colo.

The publicity department of White Stag Manufacturing Co., in Portland, Ore., entrusted me with their wonderful collection of antique ski clothes, photos of which appear in the clothing chapter. For this a special thanks to Pat Hartley and Barbara Sahli of White Stag. Fred Langendorf of Slalom Skiwear in Newport, Vt., was very helpful with items from his company.

I am very grateful to Dr. Frank Howard of San Rafael, Calif., for permitting me to use photos from his vast collection. John Jay of Rancho Santa Fe, Calif., sent photos and of course provided an inspiration with his own pictorial history book, *Ski Down the Years.*

Mary MacKenzie, historian of Lake Placid, N.Y., provided extensive research and photos of that famous ski area, while A.J. McKenna, a resident of Denver and a member of the 10th Mountain Division Association, gave photos and much information on his renowned World War II outfit.

Richard Moulton of Huntington, Vt., producer of a great movie on ski history, *Legends of American Skiing,* helped me with photographs and addresses. Gregg Sowder of Riblet Tramway Co., Spokane, Wash., permitted me to look through his extensive files on ski areas and chairlift projects. The staff of the National Ski Patrol System office in Denver was extremely helpful with both information and photos, as was the staff at the Denver Art Museum in giving me photos of the museum's 1984 display on ski clothing and equipment.

Many of the ski-area photos were obtained from the extensive archives of the U.S. Forest Service in Roslyn, Va. William Hauser assisted me in finding these photos, and I also received aid from the information officers at several of the Forest Service's regional offices.

To the public relations staffs of the many, many ski areas that provided information and photos, a sincere thanks. They are too numerous to list.

And finally, I am indebted to the following archives, organizations, individuals, and companies: state archives in California, Wyoming, Montana, Idaho, Colorado, New Mexico, Arizona, New Hampshire, Vermont, Maine, Michigan, Wisconsin, Minnesota, the Oregon State Library, University of Washington Special Collections, Western History Department of the Denver Public Library, Chicago Historical Society, NASTAR, North Carolina High Country Host, Hart Ski Co., Salomon Inc., U.S. Army Military History Institute, U.S. Army Archives, *SKI* magazine, Bill Berry, Hjalmar Hvam, John B. Allen, Rachael Simpson, who modeled the ski clothing and the Missoula City-County Library. I apologize to anyone I may have overlooked.

Mary Beth Percival, a Missoula artist, did a great job on the cover art work.

PHOTO CREDITS

CHS—Colorado Historical Society, Denver
CSM—Colorado Ski Museum and Hall of Fame, Vail, Colo.
DAM—Denver Art Museum
DPL—Denver Public Library, Western History Department
FH—Dr. Frank Howard collection, San Rafael, Calif.
LC—Library of Congress, Washington, D.C.
NA—National Archives, Washington, D.C.
NESM—New England Ski Museum, Franconia, N.H.
NSM—National Ski Hall of Fame and Museum, Ishpeming, Mich.
SV—Sun Valley Co., Sun Valley, Idaho
USA—U.S. Army Archives, Washington, D.C.
USAMHI—United States Army Military History Institute, Carlisle, Pa.
USFS—United States Forest Service Archives
WASM—Western America SkiSport Museum, Boreal Ridge, Calif.
WS—White Stag Manufacturing Co., Portland, Ore.
10th Mountain Division Assoc.
Other photographs are credited to their sources.

*This book is dedicated to Bill Berry, Dr. Frank Howard, John Jay,
the ski museums and all the others who have kept alive
the history of the great sport of downhill skiing.*

Dr. Lawton, who introduced Dartmouth Outing Club founder Fred Harris to skiing in the early 1900s. The club was at the forefront in establishing downhill skiing and racing to the U.S. NESM

Carl Nelson and Margaret Thompson, two members of the Chicago-based Norge Ski Club. The club was founded in the early 1900s by Carl Howelsen, a Norwegian jumper who came to this country and performed for the Barnum and Bailey Circus. 1923.

CHAPTER ONE

LONG BOARDS, FAST DOPE, STRAIGHT SCHUSSES

CALIFORNIA'S GOLD-RUSH SKIERS

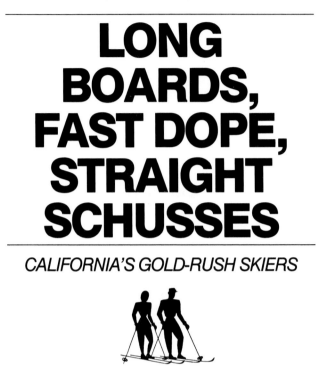

Snowshoe Thompson in the High Sierras. WASM

The history of downhill skiing in America begins during the mid-19th century in California's Sierra Mountains. It was there that a crew of gold miners, obviously afflicted with both a pronounced wild streak and a severe case of cabin fever, decided to hold downhill ski races to liven up the long winters. They had names like "Cornish Bob" Oliver, Napoleon "Little Corporal" Normandin, Peter "French Pete" Riendeau, "Quicksilver" Handel, and John Gray "Gray Flash" Pollard, and they charged straight down the mountainsides at speeds in the neighborhood of 70 and 80 miles per hour in pursuit of cash prizes and the champion's title.

Skis, of course, had been used long before the advent of the Sierra speed tourneys. Skis as old as 4,000 years have been found in the Scandinavian countries, and literary references to skiing in Europe's far north can be found as far back as Virgil's Aeneid. Likewise, some historians believe that skis first came to North America with Leif Eriksson and company about 1000 AD.

Unlike the California version, this ancient skiing did not involve much—if any—downhill running. Skiing then was basically a form of transportation over deep snows, more on a par with modern cross-country skiing. It was particularly widespread in Scandinavia, where skis were used both in peace and in war. During the Norwegian Civil War in 1206, for example, two scouts on skis carried the king's infant son over the mountains, an event that is memorialized in the annual Birkebeinerrenet cross-country ski race, named after the birch leggings the scouts wore.

With the strong Scandinavian tradition of skiing, it's no surprise that it was Scandinavian immigrants who brought skiing to the United States. The first recorded use of skis in this country occurred in 1841 in Beloit, Wis., not far from Chicago, in a region that was then being settled by Scandinavians. In the pioneer Midwest, as in Europe, skis were used for transportation, not for downhill running—for instance, there are accounts of the early Norwegian settlers in Wisconsin using skis to hunt deer.

Robert "Cornish Bob" Oliver of Sawpit Flat won the 1867 championship races held at La Porte, Calif., becoming, in effect, America's first downhill ski champion. WASM

-1-

It was the Norwegians, too, who brought skiing to California, where it evolved (at least locally) into a downhill sport. Lured by gold during the rush of '49, the immigrants found that, come winter, the High Sierra mining camps were blanketed by 10 or 15 feet of snow. Skis, or "Norwegian snowshoes" as they were known, were the only effective means of getting around.

No one knows who first introduced skiing to the Sierras, but the most famous of the early California skiers was the legendary John A. "Snowshoe" Thompson. In 1837, at the age of 10, Thompson (or Thomson) left his native Norway and in 1851 he arrived in California to join the gold miners. Instead of panning, he ended up ranching or cutting wood (accounts differ) in the Sacramento Valley.

At the time, communications between the east and west sides of the Sierra Mountains were cut off each winter due to deep snows. Familiar with skiing from his Norwegian upbringing, Thompson felled an oak tree, crafted a 25-pound pair of skis, and on Jan. 3, 1856, struck out east over the mountains from Placerville. He made the 90 miles to Genoa in the Carson Valley on the far side of the mountains, and returned to Placerville on Jan. 18. The return trip took only three and one-half days, a feat that was considered remarkable.

During the next 15 or 20 years, Snowshoe Thompson carried mail many times over this route and others. Sometimes he'd haul as much as 100 pounds on his back, up mountain and down, winding through forests and pushing through blizzards. During the winters of the early 1860s, he was the only land link between California and the rest of the nation. But eventually, Thompson's services were replaced by the railroad and stage, and in 1872 he claimed that the U.S. government owed him $5,000 for his years of mail carrying. He did not collect.

Snowshoe Thompson, the mail carrier who became America's first skiing legend, negotiating a Sierra mountainside on his "Norwegian snowshoes."   WASM

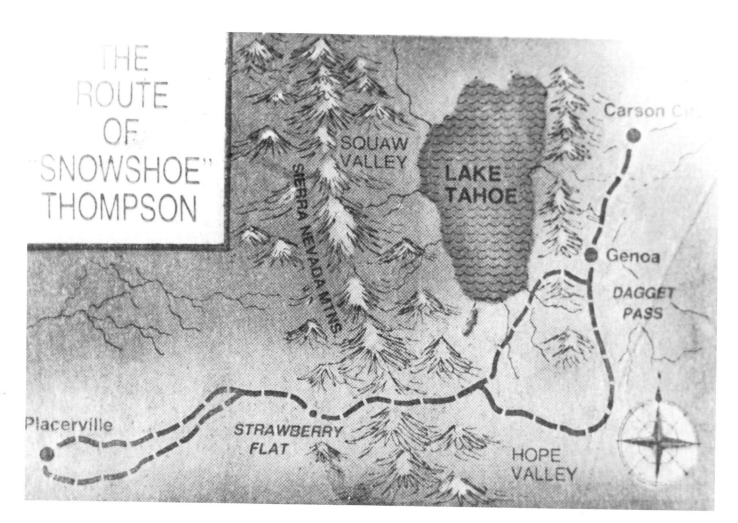

THE ROUTE OF "SNOWSHOE" THOMPSON

SQUAW VALLEY

LAKE TAHOE

Carson Ci

SIERRA NEVADA MTNS

Genoa

DAGGET PASS

Placerville

STRAWBERRY FLAT

HOPE VALLEY

Thompson in his later years. The mailbag he holds is now on display at the Western America SkiSport Museum in California.   WASM

The grave of John A. "Snowshoe" Thompson (also spelled Thomson), at Genoa, Nev. Pictured is Carl Messelt, one of America's first instructors and a pioneer of modern skiing.   FH

Meanwhile, the use of "Norwegian snowshoes" spread through the Sierra mining camps. In 1859, for example, a letter writer described how inhabitants of the region got around in the deep Sierra snows: "Nearly all have Norwegian snow shoes, about nine feet long, four and one half inches wide, shaved thin and turned up in front like a sled runner . . . with a pole in the hands for balance, a person can run over the light and new fallen snow at railroad speed." These snowshoes, it should be noted, were used not just by the miners, but by many other inhabitants of the Sierra settlements, such as children, who used them to travel to school, and doctors who made house calls on skis.

The Sierra winters, of course, were very long, and the mining camp amusements—aside from drinking and the occasional fistfight—were few. To break the monotony, someone, somewhere, came up with the bright idea of holding "snowshoe races." This was not transportation, this was sport. *Downhill* sport.

The first matchups, held about 1860, were informal affairs, but soon the races became major events, hotly contested. The various mining camps organized teams and challenged each other on courses that went straight down the open Sierra mountainsides and were lined with hundreds of wagering spectators. The racers started en masse at the sound of a gong, and they aimed their boards at a finish line marked by American flags and portable bars.

The speeds were impressive, even by today's standards: 37 seconds for a half-mile course; 17 seconds for 1,900 feet; Tommy Todd's record run in 1874 of 14 seconds down an icy 1,804-foot course, which translates to a speed of 88 miles per hour.

To achieve speeds like this, the racers worked fanatically on technique and equipment. They developed grooved skis as long as 12 feet, fastened with leather straps and carefully coated with "dope," the strange and secret mixtures they used to "wax" the long boards. The racers invented a low crouch to fight wind resistance, and they slowed themselves down by dragging their single pole, aided by a mercifully long outrun beyond the finish. Turning was strictly optional, if not impossible.

La Porte was the center of California's "snowshoe" (ski) racing in the 1860s. On race days, the Union Hotel would be packed with racers, coaches, "dopemen," and sponsors. It has been called the world's first ski hostel.   WASM

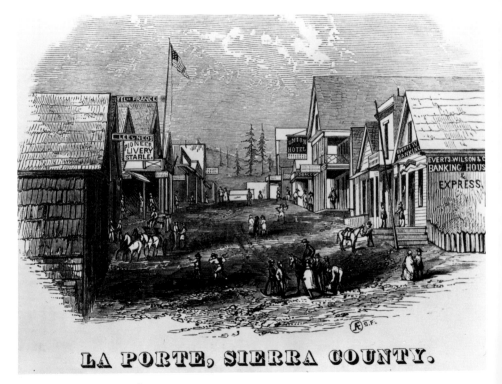

LA PORTE, SIERRA COUNTY.

THE DOPEMEN

Some of the posters advertising the Sierra "snowshoe" races of the 1860s carried the bold-lettered proclamation that "DOPE IS KING." This was not a reference to some mind-altering substance (the racers preferred their courage in liquid form); rather, it described the importance of waxing in these early-day ski races.

Dope was first introduced in Sierra and Plumas counties about 1854 as a way to increase speed and prevent snow from sticking to the skis. As the snowshoe racing craze grew, the dope and the "dopemen" who brewed and applied it became increasingly significant factors in competition, largely because the race courses demanded pure, straight-on speed to the exclusion of any turning technique. A common greeting among racers was "What dope do you use?" rather than "Hello" or "How's your family?"

One of the original dopemen was Bill Clinch of Sawpit, who cooked up a concoction of spermaceti, burgundy pitch, canada pitch, barbary tallow, camphor, castor oil, and other ingredients. The recipes for most dopes were well guarded secrets, and they came with names like Skedaddle, Greased Lightning, Slip Easy, Catch'em Quick, Breakneck, and Slip Up. The finer brands were described as "double-distilled, extra-refined, chainlightning dope." If these were half as fast as advertised, they were very fast indeed.

The man "doping" (waxing) the long skis is Frank Steward who, from 1865 to 1911, was a legendary racer, dopemaker, and coach of winning racers.   WASM

"Doping up" before the start of competition. Many races were won or lost as a result of these strange and secret mixtures.
WASM

This photo, remarkable both for its early date and its bizarre action, shows racers clowning it up at Howland Flat. The occasional crash clearly was not unknown to the early-day skiers.

California State Library

The snowshoe racers developed a low crouch—a forerunner of the modern tuck—to cut wind resistance while they were making their long straight schusses to the finish. WASM

SNOW SHOE RACES!

FOUR DAYS SNOW-SHOE RACING AT
HOWLAND FLAT,

UNDER THE AUSPICES OF THE

TABLE ROCK SNOW-SHOE CLUB,

Commencing on Monday, March 15th, '69.

PROGRAMME.

First Day. 1st Race. Club Purse of $125 free for all. 2d Race. Entrance money of the day free for all but winner of the first race
Second Day. Club Purse of $75, free for all. 2d Race. Entrance money, free for all but winner of the first race of this day.
Third Day. Club Purse $75, free for all. 2d Race. Entrance money, free for all but the winner of the first of this day.
Fourth Day. 1st race, Club Purse of $125 free for all. 2d race. Entrance money free for all but winner of first race this day.

Purses for Boys will be made up during the races. Racing to commence at precisely 1 o'clock. All entries must be made before 11 o'clock A. M. with the Secretary. Entrance fee $1. If the weather should prove unfavorable on Monday, March 15th, the Races will be postponed from day to day until favorable.

FREE DANCES DURING THE WEEK
and a GRAND BALL on St. Patricks Night

the 17th inst. at the SIERRA NEVADA HOTEL. During the week of the races the Sanhedrim of the Ancient and Honorable Order of E. C. V. located at Howland Flat, will, by permission granted by the G. R. N. H., have a celebration, procession etc.
By order of the Club.

Sam. Wheeler, Secretary.   D. H. OSBORN, President.

The Sierra races were major events. Newspaper ad for an 1869 race.
WASM

Races of all sorts were held—"Tom Thumb" races for children, races for Chinese laborers, and ladies' races, which posed special problems. To prevent their voluminous skirts from flying up over their heads, the ladies had to stand upright, a position of much greater wind resistance. One ladies' race was easily won by a woman who adopted the men's crouch, using the pole to clutch her skirts below her knees.

La Porte was both a commercial center of the mining district and the hub of snowshoe racing, boasting several hotels as well as 14 saloons. By 1867, racing had become so popular that La Porte skiers organized the Alturas Snowshoe Club, which formalized racing rules, sponsored tournaments, and was perhaps the world's first ski club—actually more of a ski association—devoted to racing. That year, the club put on its first annual tournament, which could be considered North America's first downhill ski championships. At about the same time, in Europe, the first formal jumping and cross-country competitions were getting underway.

Racers making the long climb to the top of the course, decades before the invention of the ski lift. Unconfirmed reports, however, claim that some early Sierra skiers rode up in the ore buckets that serviced the mines.   WASM

Racing at La Porte.
Author's collection

A group of would-be racers at La Porte, 1897.   WASM

Snowshoeing wasn't just racing. In the High Sierra settlements, winter transportation was dependent on snowshoes. Travel from town to town was via a network of ski trails, and doctors even made house calls on skis.   WASM

The ladies too with modest grace,
Will take their chance to win
    the race;
Their hearts may beat with fear
    or hope,
But each has got her lightning
    "Dope"—
The signals given, off they go;
Pull wild at starting, scratching
    snow,
And if the dears are not experts,
The air seems filled with snow
    and skirts.

They try again, with faces aglow,
determined to win or die in
    the snow.

                    By a miner, 1879

Children competed in "Tom Thumb" races, which were one event in tournaments that lasted several days and served as family social gatherings.   WASM

Women skiers in Vermont.
Vermont Historical Society

Skiers at Atlanta, Idaho, with Greylock Mountain in the background.
Idaho Historical Society

Ski group at Ivers, Idaho.
Idaho Historical Society

The first La Porte races, drawing competitors from throughout the region, lasted three days and featured purses ranging from $25 to $75, including a prize for the ladies. Over 40 skiers, representing several different teams, competed for the silver-studded belt that would go to the winner of the championship event, held on a 1,230-foot course. In this event, "Cornish Bob" Oliver and John G. Pollard, both from Sawpit Flat, tied with a time of 14 seconds, and, in a tie-breaker race, Cornish Bob aced out Pollard by a distance of four feet. The racers and fans then marched off to a ball at La Porte's Masonic Hall.

It was at the third annual La Porte championship that Snowshoe Thompson, by then a legend, met his match. Thompson, who traveled 200 miles to attend, was an expert at skiing the backcountry—at turning to avoid obstacles and running up and down hills. The La Porte crowd, in contrast, knew only one maneuver—full speed, straight ahead—which was all they needed to negotiate their courses. Thompson knew nothing about "dope" and the aerodynamic crouch; predictably, he lost, failing even to cross the finish line during the first race.

Obviously sporting a badly bruised ego, Thompson then challenged the La Porte racers to a rematch the following winter that would include, among other things, jumping and a run "from the top to the bottom of the highest and heaviest timbered mountain we can find." He showed nothing but disdain for their straight-running, their dope, and their "squat," while the La Porte racers, in turn, regarded his upright style as effeminate.

The La Porte crowd never did take up the challenge, but the repercussions from that third annual La Porte championship echoed for years. In 1874, an item in La Porte's local newspaper noted that Thompson's skis had gone on public display over in Carson City. The editor couldn't refrain from tacking a comment onto the bottom of the item: "Wonder if these are the same shoes that he brought to La Porte to beat the L.P. boys some years ago. If we remember rightly he went home with a large sized bug in his ear and concluded he didn't know the first principles of handling the 'Greased Boards.'"

The last La Porte race was held in 1911; by that time the gold had played out, the mining camps had faded, and "snowshoe" racing was largely a thing of the past. But in the meantime, skiing had been introduced to other areas of the United States, at first purely as a practical means of transportation. As early as the 1850s, a minister, doubling as a mail carrier, was using skis in the Colorado Rockies, and a decade later in Iowa they were used for the same purpose. Then, in the 1880s, skiing took on a sporting component when Scandinavian immigrants (again) introduced ski jumping to the northern areas of Michigan, Wisconsin, Minnesota, and New England, places where it grew into a popular spectator sport. In the 1880s, recreational skiers began to pop up elsewhere—in 1885, a group of railroad engineers formed a ski club in Pennsylvania, and four years later, during the blizzard of 1889, a man skied down New York City's Broadway.

The winter of 1904-05 saw the advent of what was probably the nation's first winter sports and ski resort when the Lake Placid Club, a summer sporting club in upstate New York, decided to stay open for the winter season, offering skiing in addition to a number of other activities. Also in 1904, a group of Midwestern jumpers met at Ishpeming, Mich., to form America's first national ski organization. Five years later, Fred Harris founded the Dartmouth Outing Club in Hanover, N.H., which would pioneer intercollegiate ski competition and do much to promote skiing in the East, while Norwegian champion jumper Carl Howelsen was introducing the sport to Colorado. In 1913, back in California, skiers started using a primitive uphill lift—probably the nation's first—at Truckee, which even then was being promoted as a winter sports resort.

By this time, skiing as a sport—rather than as a form of transportation—essentially had been established in the United States. It grew bit by bit in little pockets around the country, and by the mid-1930s, in the aftermath of the widely publicized 1932 Winter Olympics at Lake Placid, the sport was in the grip of a boom.

Members of the Norden Ski Club, based in Ishpeming, Mich., late 1800s. Founded by jumpers, the Norden Ski Club was one of the nation's first.   NSM

Skiing remained late in Alaska, and for good reason. This photo is titled "May Day in the Northland"; it shows ice hummocks in the Bering Sea opposite Nome, Alaska, 1910.
University of Alaska Archives

Skiers at Nome, Alaska.
University of Alaska Archives

A skiing family at Steamboat Springs, Colo.   CHS

Snowshoers (skiers) in Gunnison County, Colo., March 1883. Skis were used by mailmen in Colorado as early as the 1850s.   DPL

Skiers on a hill at Lund Ranch, north of Dillon, Colo., 1912.   DPL

One of the earliest portrayals of skiing in the Rocky Mountains is this 1865 painting of a skier approaching Fort Owen in the Bitterroot Valley of the Montana Territory. It was painted by Peter Petersen Tofft and reproduced in THE JOURNALS AND LETTERS OF MAJOR JOHN OWEN, PIONEER OF THE NORTHWEST, 1850-1870.

Museum of Fine Arts, Boston, Mass.

Skiing in the Colorado mountains.
CHS

Skiers near Battle, Wyo., 1904.   Wyoming State Archives

F. Jay Haynes, a well-known early Western photographer, spent many years recording the sights of Yellowstone National Park. Here he poses on skis inside his studio at Bozeman, Mont., 1894.

Montana Historical Society
Haynes photo

Skiers waxing at Hyalite Canyon, near Bozeman, Mont., late 1800s.   Museum of the Rockies,
Bozeman, Mont.

Skiing party at Upper Geyser Basin, Yellowstone National Park, January 1887. Yellowstone has become popular with today's cross-country skiers.
Montana Historical Society
Haynes photo

In 1894, F. Jay Haynes led a winter excursion into Yellowstone Park, making much of the journey on skis. Members of the party had to remove their skis to cross Alum Creek.   Montana Historical Society
Haynes photo

Cabin at the Mud Volcano, Yellowstone National Park, 1894.
Montana Historical Society
Haynes photo

Early day skiers at Mount Rainier, Wash.   U. of Washington Special Collections

Early day jumpers in Michigan.   Author's collection

THE SNOW-SHOE RACES

WHEN SNOW LIES DEEP ON EVERY HILL,
SILENCE REIGNS, THE BIRDS ARE STILL;
WHERE GOLD IS NESTLING IN THE MINES,
AND DARK CLEFTS REST AMONG THE PINES;
THE EARTH IS ROBED IN PUREST WHITE,
THE SUN GIVES OUT ITS DAZZLING LIGHT;
THE SNOW-SHOE RACERS EACH IN PLACE,
THE GIVEN SIGNAL STARTS THE RACE.

PEOPLE IN CITIES NEVER CAN KNOW
HOW JOLLY IT IS TO GLIDE O'ER THE SNOW.

THE LADIES TOO WITH MODEST GRACE,
WILL TAKE THEIR CHANCE TO WIN THE RACE;
THEIR HEARTS MAY BEAT WITH FEAR OR HOPE,
BUT EACH HAS GOT HER LIGHTNING ''DOPE'' --
THE SIGNAL'S GIVEN, OFF THEY GO;
PULL WILD AT STARTING, SCRATCHING SNOW,
AND IF THE DEARS ARE NOT EXPERTS,
THE AIR SEEMS FILLED WITH SNOW AND SKIRTS.

THEY TRY IT AGAIN, WITH FACES AGLOW,
DETERMINED TO WIN OR DIE IN THE SNOW.

DOWN THE MOUNTAIN SIDE, LIKE BIRDS IN FLIGHT,
OR METEORS ON A STARRY NIGHT --
BENDING LOW TO MISS THE BREEZE,
FLYING PAST THE STATELY TREES,
RUSHING DOWN TO THE FLAT BELOW,
DANCING OVER THE ''BEAUTIFUL SNOW,''
FALLING, ROLLING, SEEING STARS ---
THEN HEAR THE LAUGHING CROWD'S HURRAHS.

AWAY DOWN THE VALLEYS, WHERE ORANGES GROW,
THEY MISS ALL THE FUN WE HAVE IN THE SNOW.

WHEN DARKNESS O'ER THE HILLS ADVANCE,
THE SPORT ENDS WITH THE SOCIAL DANCE;
CHILL WINTER THUS HIS PLEASURES BRING,
AND WATER FLOWS WITH EARLY SPRING,
THE GLITTERING GOLD THAT LAY BELOW,
IS BROUGHT TO LIGHT BY MELTING SNOW;
THE TRACK IS GONE, BUT BEAMING FACES
WITH GLEE RECALL THE SNOW-SHOE RACES.

PEOPLE IN CITIES AND VALLEYS MAY KNOW,
WHEN IT'S FALLING THERE'S GOLD IN THE SNOW.

—MINER

(MOUNTAIN MESSENGER, FEBRUARY 1, 1879)

CHAPTER TWO

GETTING ORGANIZED

EARLY SKI ORGANIZATIONS

Between the heyday of the Sierra miners' races in the mid-1800s and the nationwide boom in downhill skiing in the 1930s, the American ski scene was dominated by Nordic skiers—especially by jumpers, many of them Scandinavian immigrants working in the forests and mines of the northern U.S. These were the men who, in 1904 (some accounts say 1901), founded America's first national ski organization.

The roots of the organization go back to Ishpeming, a town in Upper Michigan's iron-mining country. The town had held its first jumping meet in 1888, and, like many other communities in the Upper Midwest, Ishpeming boasted a ski club whose purpose was to promote jumping and organize competitions.

After several successful jumping tournaments were held in Ishpeming during the early years of the 20th century, a group of Norwegian-born jumpers, along with local newspaper editor George Newett, met one evening in the Ishpeming office of Carl Tellefsen. A local banker who had immigrated in 1887 from Trondheim, Norway, Tellefsen had made his first Ishpeming jump in 1888. (He flew 42 feet, 6 inches, according to a newspaper account, and possessed an "elegant" style.)

In Tellefsen's office that night, the men founded the National Ski Association of America (NSA), with Tellefsen elected its first president. Its purpose was to conduct jumping tournaments and set standards that participating clubs would follow. The Ishpeming Ski Club had scheduled a jumping tournament for the day following the meeting, and this competition, receiving the sanctioning of the new organization, became the first annual National Ski Jumping Tournament, held on Feb. 22, 1904.

From that time, the organization sanctioned an annual national championship, and more and more clubs joined its ranks. Initially, jumping tournaments like these were professional events, with cash prizes awarded to the winners, but at the 1922 annual convention in Chicago, the NSA withdrew its sanction from professional tournaments.

In the 1920s, the NSA began to attract affiliate divisions. In 1925 it gained an affiliate in the Eastern Amateur Ski Association, which had been founded in 1922 at the Berkeley Hotel in Saranac Lake, N.Y.; in 1926, the Western U.S. Ski Association (later split into several parts) became a national affiliate; in 1928 the Central Division, organized a year earlier in Minneapolis, joined the ranks; and in 1930 the California Ski Association was organized, being admitted to the national group the same year, as was the Pacific Northwest Division. Much later, in 1963, came the Alaska Division, and in 1972 the Southern Division.

George Newett, editor and publisher of the ISHPEMING IRON ORE and a founder of the National Ski Association. He is recognized as "the man who Americanized the skisport." NSM

Carl Tellefsen, the chief organizer of the National Ski Association and its first president.   NSM

Aksel Holter, one of the founders of the National Ski Association and president of the association from 1904-09. He also was editor of the American Ski Annual and a jumping competitor.   NSM

From the beginning, the Eastern Amateur was an especially strong group. Its original member clubs included Brattleboro of Vermont, Nansen of Berlin, N.H., the Norsemen of New York City, the Saranac Lake Ski Club, the Sno Birds of Lake Placid, and the Dartmouth Outing Club.

All through its early years, the NSA concentrated on ski jumping, but as early as 1925 the Eastern Amateur was pushing for the recognition of Alpine competition, which at the time was a new event and was seen primarily in intercollegiate competitions. By 1933, the NSA had adopted Alpine competition, sanctioning its first national downhill championships that year at Mount Moosilauke, N.H.

The Eastern group—and especially its president, Harry Wade Hicks of Lake Placid—also was instrumental in sending a U.S. ski team to the 1928 Olympics in St. Moritz, thereby helping to pave the way for the 1932 Olympics at Lake Placid, and it was Eastern that provided some of the initial push in the formation of the National Ski Patrol System.

As the years went by, and downhill skiing grew, the NSA sanctioned more Alpine competitions. Its first national slalom championships were held in 1935 at Mount Rainier; the first women's Alpine national championships were held in 1938 at Stowe, and Reno's Slide Mountain was the site of the first giant slalom championships in 1949.

Now under the name the United States Ski Association, the organization is headquartered in Colorado Springs, Colo., and is the governing body for competitive skiing in the United States.

FIRST RACING CLUB

"This is to let the world and the balance of creation know that the members of the Alturas Snow-Shoe Club do hereby agree and bind themselves to furnish a man to compete with anybody that's 'ON IT' in the snow-shoe line for any sum of money from $1,000 to $100,000."
—An 1867 advertisement in the "Mountain Messenger"

Starting about 1860, according to ski historian Bill Berry, the Sierra gold miners began organizing small clubs and committees which oversaw "snowshoe" races. These were informal organizations. The Alturas Snowshoe Club of La Porte, writes Berry, was "the Sierra's very first ski club organized for the specific purpose of staging championship events." In 1867, the year of its founding, the club sponsored its first downhill championships, won by Sawpit's "Cornish Bob" Oliver.

This first ski club was not exactly a self-effacing organization, as is seen in the 1867 advertisement the club placed in the local "Mountain Messenger" (above). But the Alturas skiers were very fast as well as very proud; they earned their bragging rights. After Alturas skiers humiliated Snowshoe Thompson in the La Porte championships in 1869, the acting president of the Alturas club, responding to Thompson's challenge for a rematch, issued the following statement:

"This fellow talks about La Porters not 'having a right to be called scientific snowshoe riders.' Why, Doc. Brewster has a mule that has been practicing this winter on snowshoes, that can beat him on an even string, and we have Chinamen that can discount him."

DARTMOUTH OUTING CLUB

The Dartmouth Outing Club was at the forefront in establishing Alpine ski competition in the United States, and it also did much to encourage the growth of skiing in general.

The club was founded in 1909 when Fred Harris, an undergraduate at Dartmouth College in Hanover, N.H., proposed that students form a club to take advantage of winter, which in those years was a season that most people—Dartmouth students included—spent indoors.

The idea was well received, and that winter the club held its first "Winter meet," the forerunner to the famous Dartmouth Winter Carnival. The club, which offered activities in all seasons, grew in the next few years, and started to construct trails and cabins in the New Hampshire woods. It also organized outings, such as winter ski ascents in the Presidential Mountains led by Fred Harris.

In 1913 Dartmouth traveled to McGill University in Canada for America's first intercollegiate ski competition, and in 1915 Dartmouth held its own first intercollegiate competition during the Winter Carnival, with skiers in attendance from McGill, the University of New Hampshire, University of Vermont, and Williams College.

These early competitions featured only Nordic ski events, but in the 1920s Alpine racing arrived. Some of those with an early interest in Alpine competition were Dartmouth Professor C.A. Proctor and his son, C.N. Proctor, who competed in the 1928 Winter Olympics and was the first to ski the Headwall at Tuckerman's Ravine.

The elder Proctor in 1923 set the nation's first between-the-poles slalom course, and in 1928 organized the world's first slalom that was run under modern FIS rules. Dartmouth also held the nation's first modern downhill, run in 1927 on the Mount Moosilauke Carriage Road.

Meanwhile, the Dartmouth ski teams grew steadily in power. In the 1930s, under coaches Otto Schniebs and later Walter Prager, they dominated U.S. Alpine racing. Dick Durrance, the nation's top pre-war racer, was a Dartmouth skier, as were Ted Hunter, A.F. Washburn, and Warren Chivers, who, along with Durrance, were members of the 1936 U.S. Olympic team.

After the war, Denver University eventually established dominance of U.S. intercollegiate racing, but Dartmouth continued to produce top skiers—among them Olympic Alpine skiers Colin Stewart, Bill Beck, Ralph Miller, Brooks Dodge, Chiharu Igaya, David Lawrence, Tom Corcoran, and David Currier. Dartmouth was represented at the 1984 Games in Sarajevo by Tiger Shaw, class of '85.

Fred Harris, who in 1909 founded the Dartmouth Outing Club. NESM

THE AUBURN SKI CLUB

The Auburn Ski Club of California is one of the West's oldest and most active ski organizations. Like many of the early ski clubs, it originally focused on ski jumping, although later it was instrumental in introducing Alpine competition to California.

The club was founded in 1928 "to provide warm shelter, cleared slopes, and the first engineered ski jumping hill to be built in California," according to a club history. In 1931, Auburn acquired land near Cisco for jumping facilities, but had to convince the California legislature to keep open during the winter the highway that led to the area. At Winter Park, as the area was called, the club built a number of jumping hills, including California's largest.

This facility helped develop a long line of top ski jumpers, among them the legendary Roy Mikkelsen (twice national champion), as well as Sig Vettestad, Halvor Mikkelsen (an all-around skier), and Rolf Wigaard. The club also sponsored jumping tournaments in the San Francisco Bay Area, on the theory that it was easier to bring the snow to the spectators (via railroad cars) than to bring the spectators to the snow. Its 1934 San Francisco Ski Jumping Championships attracted 100,000 spectators, according to some estimates, and in 1939 it hosted the World Open Ski Jumping Championships in the Bay Area.

The Auburn Ski Club has a number of firsts to its name: Auburn's Wendell Robie was first president of the California Ski Association, formed in 1931; in 1933 the club sponsored California's first Alpine competition (a year later at Winter Park's Tunnel Mountain it built the state's second ski tow); and in 1940, the club staged the nation's first military ski patrol race, which combined shooting and skiing.

After World War II, an interstate highway project resulted in the condemnation of the original Auburn ski area, and the club acquired land at Boreal Ridge, near the summit of Donner Pass. There the ski club currently maintains a jumping hill (named in honor of Roy Mikkelsen), as well as cross-country and Alpine racing facilities. At Boreal Ridge the club also has built the Auburn Ski Club Chapel and the Western America SkiSport Museum.

Left: Charles (Charley) N. Proctor, Dartmouth '28 (left), his father, Charles A. Proctor, Dartmouth '00 (middle) and German (Gerry) Raab (right), coach of the Dartmouth ski team. This photo was taken by Nelson Rockefeller, Dartmouth '30, on Jan. 20, 1928, the day before Charley left for the Olympics.
Robert Baumrucker

Right: Both Proctors would make many contributions to the ski world in the East and West. This is a later photo of Charley, who made the 1928 Olympic team. He was in charge of ski trail design for the U.S. Forest Service in New Hampshire, coached the Harvard ski team, and in 1938 became director of ski operations at California's Yosemite National Park, a post he held for 20 years. He also was prominent in the California Ski Association as an officer and official, and as a member of the 1960 Olympic Ski Advisory Committee.

Charles A. Proctor was a professor of physics at Dartmouth and a leader in early ski racing in the East; his contributions included his active support of the 1924 and 1928 Olympic teams and serving as an officer at the 1932 Lake Placid Games.　　　NSM

CHAPTER THREE

BACK TO THE BASICS

SKI INSTRUCTION AND TECHNIQUE

A 1922 telemark turn by Lieutenant Albizzi, Colorado. Invented in Norway in the mid-19th century, the telemark was the first effective method of turning a pair of skis.   DPL

Fixed firmly in the American consciousness is the image of the ski instructor—a handsome, bronzed expert with a soft Austrian accent and gracious manners. Unlike many such images, however, this one has its basis in fact—it was the Europeans who pioneered and for decades dominated ski instruction in the United States. At times, it seemed, sending instructors to America was a major export industry for countries like Austria and Switzerland. And if they were not always handsome and gracious, the foreign instructors did know how to ski.

In a sense, the exodus to America began about 150 years ago in Norway. It was there that a young skier named Sondre Norheim invented the first effective method of turning a pair of skis. The turn consisted of sliding one foot forward until the tip of one ski was near the boot of the other. The forward ski was then turned in the desired direction, leading the skier through the turn like a rudder.

Norheim's turn, which bears a resemblance to genuflection, took its name from the inventor's hometown—Telemark. Meanwhile, also in Norway, other skiers were experimenting with keeping their skis approximately parallel and skidding them through a turn. This maneuver was named for another Norwegian town—Christiania.

But the Norwegians were interested primarily in jumping and cross-country, not downhill skiing. The next significant development in downhill technique took place in the Alps, where skiing began to catch on in the late 19th century.

Near Lilienfeld, Austria, not far from Vienna, lived a man by the name of Mathias Zdarsky, who has been described as something of an eccentric hermit. Zdarsky read a book by explorer Fridtjof Nansen, who in 1888 had crossed the Greenland ice cap on skis, and Zdarsky decided that skis might offer a means of getting into town during winter. He ordered a pair, but having no instructions in their use, he was forced to develop his own ski technique. In 1892, he founded the first ski school in Europe.

HANNES SCHNEIDER

Hannes Schneider, founder of the Arlberg ski technique and the great St. Anton ski school. With its emphasis on stem turns, the Arlberg method replaced the telemark turn. NESM

Hannes Schneider, pioneer of the first widely used ski technique, was born in 1890 in Stuben, Austria. He learned to ski at a young age with the help of a man named Viktor Sohm, who taught him a rudimentary snowplow and stem.

Schneider's father hoped he'd become a cheese maker, but in 1907 the young Schneider took a job as ski teacher at the Hotel Post in St. Anton, striking a deal with his father to do so—if, after the first season, he didn't make money teaching, he would be apprenticed to a cheese maker.

Apparently he turned a profit, for Schneider stayed at St. Anton and revolutionized the ski world with his creation, the "Arlberg method." The technique was systematic, leading the skier through the snowplow, the stem turn, stem christiania, and on to parallel swing turns.

Winning converts to his method was not always easy. Once at a race in St. Moritz, then a stronghold of the telemark, Schneider found himself defending his new method. Unbeknownst to the racers, who hadn't seen the course, they would be forced to jump a bare road and stone wall, whereupon, much to the amusement of the spectators, they would be flying toward a large water-hole.

While Schneider awaited his turn, he heard gales of laughter from down below when the other racers tried to negotiate the obstacles. Yet, when it was his turn, Schneider cleared the wall, turned his skis in mid-air, and managed to stop short of the waterhole. He went on to win the race, dealing a severe blow to the popularity of the telemark.

During World War I, Schneider served with the Austrian mountain troops, fighting against the famed Italian Alpini. For a time he and his men maintained an outpost on the top of the Koenigspitz, a peak in the Alps, where they repelled regular Italian assaults on the summit by tossing hand grenades in deep snow, thus setting off avalanches that would sweep the slopes below. The most fearsome attacks, however, came from lightning bolts, which the soldiers escaped by burrowing deep into snow caves.

After the war, Schneider returned to St. Anton. His school began to receive world-wide recognition, in part due to his sense of the dramatic, his natural leadership ability, and his personal charisma. His methods received additional publicity when he collaborated on several ski movies with German filmmaker Dr. Arnold Fanck.

Some of Schneider's St. Anton instructors came to the U.S. and started other Schneider ski schools; in 1939 Schneider himself came to this country after his release from Nazi jails had been arranged by American finance executive Harvey Gibson.

When, in Boston, he was first shown photos of the New Hampshire ski country, he asked where the mountains were, but he soon settled permanently in North Conway, N.H. In addition to running the Mount Cranmore ski school, he developed the first groomed slopes by cutting trees and clearing obstacles from the south side of the mountain.

Before he died in 1955, Schneider saw the popularity of his Arlberg system decline in the face of the French technique and then the new Austrian method. Nevertheless, his systematic approach to ski instruction and many of his basic maneuvers are still in use in ski schools around the world. His son Herbert continues today as director of his father's ski school at Cranmore.

Zdarsky's method became known as the Lilienfeld technique. It required a long pole (used as a brake), a low crouch, and a bit of a stem. Later, with the help of Col. Georg Bilgeri, an Austrian army officer, Zdarsky started using two poles, widened the stem, and developed the snowplow. These efforts have earned Zdarsky the title (at least in some skiers' minds) of "the father of alpine skiing."

Zdarsky may have been the first of the prominent Austrian instructors, but a man from Stuben was the more influential. His name was Hannes Schneider, and he developed what came to be known as the "Arlberg method."

As a youth, Schneider took up the new sport of skiing, and, against the wishes of his father, who hoped he'd become a cheese maker, he signed on in 1907 as a ski instructor at St. Anton. There he began to develop the technique that would dominate the skiing world.

Before Schneider's arrival, skiing, even in the Alps, was primarily regarded as a method of getting *up* a mountain rather than down. But to Schneider, the lure of skiing was downhill speed, and his techniques offered a safe and effective way to control that speed.

Essentially, Schneider seized on to Zdarsky's stem and ran with it. In the Arlberg system, the snowplow was a basic maneuver, as was the stem turn. In the stem, a skier wishing to turn to the left would push the heel of his right ski outward until the ski was pointed in the desired direction. Then the skier would transfer his weight to the "stemmed" ski.

Skiers using Schneider's system also assumed a crouch, to lower the center of gravity, and they brought their outside shoulders around in the direction of the turn (rotation). The more advanced a skier, the less he stemmed, until the skis were nearly parallel throughout a turn. Still, the stem formed the basis of Schneider's system.

After World War I, in which Schneider fought with the mountain troops against the Italians, the Hannes Schneider Ski School in St. Anton spread the Arlberg word. From this school a wave of European instructors would invade the U.S.

Other European instructors were here before them, but not many. In fact, there wasn't much instruction at all in the United States before about the mid-1930s. The nation's first organized ski school was started in 1929 at Peckett's-on-Sugar Hill, N.H. Peckett's was a distinguished summer resort, but after Katherine Peckett, daughter of the owner and a skier, visited Schneider's St. Anton school, she convinced her father to open his inn during the winter. Katherine Peckett also rounded up four Austrian instructors—first Sig Buchmayr, who was already in the U.S. on the jumping circuit, then Kurt Thalhammer, who headed the school with Buchmayr, Harold Paumgarten, and Richard Suiter.

America's first organized ski school, at Peckett's-on-
Sugar Hill, N.H.   NESM

In many ways instruction at Peckett's was a harbinger of ski instruction in America in the decades to come. Minnie Dole, writing in his memoir, *Adventures in Skiing,* describes a lesson at Peckett's in the early 1930s under the direction of Sig Buchmayr. Most of the students, including Dole, knew only two skiing maneuvers—the telemark, and running straight down. At Peckett's, however, the instructors taught the Arlberg stem. Writes Dole:

"After a round of exercises (outdoors) which Sig led ('to get der blood spinning'), we were allowed to strap on our bear-trap bindings and assume the snowplow position. There were at least fifty of us that New Year's, if I remember correctly. Pants were like as not tucked into wool socks (a few had properly baggy pre-stretch ski pants). Almost everyone wore their socks outside. But nobody cared or knew any better. It was a rollicking, laughing group. The hats took the prize. They were the most unfashionable combination of earflaps, sun visors, and flattops that could have been fitted to fifty cold heads.

"Sig took his place at the front of the flat practice area. He lined us up in four rows with about twelve square feet for each. We were ordered to spraddle the skis apart at the tails, and next came that deathless phrase, so new then and so hackneyed now, 'Bend ze knees.' Added to that, '*Nein!* Not ze back, ze knees!' "

Other than Peckett's there were a few other places to get instruction. Erling Strom, a Norwegian who, according to Lowell Thomas, was the first instructor in the nation, taught at Lake Placid; Otto Schniebs coached the boys down at Dartmouth; Hans Thorner first taught at Lake Placid, then at Mount Rainier; Hannes Schroll was at Yosemite.

The ski school at Gilbert's Hill, near Woodstock, Vt., site of the nation's first rope tow. This photo was taken in March 1940 when Sig Buchmayr had moved from Peckett's and was teaching at Woodstock with Bob Bourdon.

LC

Luggi Foeger, a man of many talents in the ski world—racer, ski school director, 10th Mountain trooper, movie director, ski area developer.   NSM

Hans Hauser.   SV

First Sun Valley Ski School, 1936-37, under the direction of Hans Hauser, former Austrian national champion.   SV

Starting about the mid-1930s, as skiing caught on in the U.S., the European instructors began to arrive in droves. Many were teachers from Hannes Schneider's St. Anton school, and they spread out through the U.S. to establish their own schools using the Arlberg method. Benno Rybizka, formerly the top instructor at St. Anton, opened a Schneider school in 1936-37 at North Conway, N.H.; Luggi Foeger taught at Yosemite; Otto Lang, later to become a movie producer, went to Mount Rainier, opening a Hannes Schneider Ski School in 1936. Friedl Pfeifer ran Sun Valley's school and later Aspen's; Sepp Ruschp taught at Stowe and was later instrumental in developing a major resort there. The Swiss came over too—among them Walter Prager, who coached at Dartmouth, and Fred Iselin, who eventually directed ski schools at Aspen.

Then, in 1939, the man himself arrived in the United States. Schneider had been arrested in St. Anton by Nazis when Germany took over Austria in 1938. Skiers all over the world protested his jailing, including Harvey Gibson, who, in addition to owning North Conway's Cranmore Mountain, was president of Manufacturer's Hanover Trust. Working through the bank's London officers, Gibson managed to get Schneider released. Schneider then moved permanently to North Conway, where, upon his arrival, he was greeted by Benno Rybizka, ringing churchbells, and an archway of ski poles raised by 150 schoolchildren.

As more resorts were established, so were more ski schools. Sun Valley (built in 1936) started its school with five Austrians, originally headed by Hans Hauser, who had been Austrian national champion three times, then by Friedl Pfeifer. Hannes Schroll took part in the discovery of the mountain that became California's Sugar Bowl ski area, and then he ran the area's ski school. Dick Durrance started the ski school at Alta, which opened its lifts in 1938. And after the war there were others—Aspen cranked up in 1946 with a ski school of four (including Friedl Pfeifer) which grossed $3,000 the first winter, while Michigan's Boyne Mountain hired Stein Eriksen (who later moved to Colorado) in 1953. Then came the Lake Tahoe resorts, along with Jackson Hole, Taos, Vail, and all the rest. The ski instruction business flourished, with a major ski school employing scores of instructors.

For years, Hannes Schneider's Arlberg technique was king, but as skiing proliferated other systems appeared, and the adherents of each method vigorously defended its merits. The Arlberg method first received a major jolt at the 1936 Olympics when Anton "Toni" Seelos foreran the slalom. Seelos kept his skis

SOME NOTABLE INSTRUCTORS

Sun Valley's ski school when Friedl Pfeifer, another former Austrian racer, was its director.   SV

Otto Lang, another of Schneider's former instructors who came to this country. In Alaska, 1940, and (right) as a movie producer.
Top: Alaska Historical Library
Right: NSM

Norwegian racer Stein Eriksen, whose graceful style became known to skiers around the world.
NSM

Sel Hannah, well-known New Hampshire ski school director.
NSM

Friedl Pfeifer.
NSM

An older Friedl Pfeifer. He went on to co-direct the ski school at Aspen, and played a major role in the development of the resort.   NSM

A later photo of Sepp Ruschp. He was instrumental in the development of Stowe as a major ski resort. NSM

Early days at Mount Mansfield and the Sepp Ruschp Ski School.
Author's Collection

Sepp Ruschp, director of the Mount Mansfield ski school at Stowe, and his "Hot Four" instructors, 1940. Left to right: Kerr Sparks, Howard Moody, Lionel Hays, Otto Hallaus, Sepp Ruschp.
Richard Moulton

totally parallel and employed shoulder rotation (swinging the shoulders in the direction of the turn). He beat the official winner, who used stem turns, by five seconds. The Arlberg stem, at least in certain circles, was out.

Emile Allais, a Frenchman, popularized a derivation of Seelos' all-parallel method, branding it the "French technique," a technique that ignored the stem. Fritz Loosli, a Swiss living in Canada, brought the all-parallel doctrine to the U.S., while back in Europe, the French skiers dominated the racing circuit during the 1940s.

But the Austrian racers, and Austrian technique, again rose to the fore when Austrians began winning with a more upright and parallel version of the old Arlberg technique. Then it became clear that when the Austrians ran a tight slalom course, they were not rotating their shoulders at all—unlike the French and old Arlbergers. Rather the racer would keep his upper body facing downhill, while his skis and lower body twisted through the turns. Some called this "delayed shoulder;" others named it "wedeln"—translated "tail-wagging."

This all was studied, refined, and systematized in the early 1950s by Stefan Kruckenhauser, professor of biology and sport at Austria's University of Innsbruck, who shot thousands of feet of film of racers making turns at St. Christoph. Kruckenhauser's system, called the "shortswing" by some, relied on parallel turns made by thrusting the heels in one direction and twisting the shoulders, as a counterforce, in the opposite direction. (An analogy was made between a skier and a man standing on a piano stool—if he twists his feet to the right, his shoulders will naturally swing to the left.) This upper body position came to be known as "reverse shoulder," or "counter-rotation," in contrast to the French and Arlberg upper body rotation, where the shoulders twisted in the same direction as the turn.

Kruckenhauser did not ignore the old Arlberg system—he borrowed from it what he needed. Thus, under Kruckenhauser, a beginning skier would first learn to traverse in a "comma" position, then learn a snowplow turn, a stem turn, a single parallel turn, and finally the quick, linked parallel turns known as wedeln. And, as instructor Hans Thorner said of the wedeln, "unless you could do it with tightly closed feet and legs, you were a slob."

Emile Allais, father of parallel ski instruction, also designed the first European metal ski, invented the quilted ski parka, coached U.S. and Canadian ski teams, and designed resorts in the U.S. and Europe. His French method of instruction shook the foundations of the Austrian's Arlberg stem-turn system.   FH

Paul Valar, ski school director at Cannon Mountain, N.H. Left to right: Paul Valar, Paula Valar, Dick Conley, Emmy Johnson, Sel Hannah, unknown.   NESM

Bill Lash, one of the founders and first president of the Professional Ski Instructors of America (PSIA). Lash has been an advocate of standardized ski instruction for many years.   NSM

Willy Shaeffler, coach of the championship Denver University ski teams, wrote a series of articles on the new ski technique in 1957 for *Sports Illustrated*. The new Austrian doctrine took hold; much of what is taught today still is based on the professor's work.

Ski instruction in the U.S. took another major step in 1961 when the Professional Ski Instructors of America (PSIA) organized in Whitefish, Mont. (1982 membership, over 14,000), and within a few years, the organization had introduced the American Ski Technique, which was based on the Austrian system. U.S. instructors, however, continued to experiment with new methods. In the early 1960s, for example, Clif Taylor of Squaw Valley developed the short ski technique (now called Graduated Length Method or GLM), in which beginners are taught on very short skis and graduate to longer models as they improve.

Another landmark in recent ski instruction was the publication of Warren Witherell's *How the Racers Ski* (1972). The book made a very emphatic distinction between a carved and a skidded turn, and soon skiers all over the nation were paying very close attention to the way their edges bit into the snow.

In Europe, too, ski technique has seen numerous refinements, innovations, and offshoots. The French, for instance, have always tended toward their own technique, with little reverse shoulder and a more square upper body. French racers, such as Jean-Claude Killy, triple-gold winner at the 1968 Olympics, popularized innovations such as "avalement" (sitting back to "swallow" bumps) and a wide-track rather than tight-footed stance.

The current American Teaching Method (ATM), as put forth in Horst Abraham's book *Skiing Right,* appears to borrow ideas from many of these different methods, blending them into a system that emphasizes a "humanistic" approach to skiing and one that employs a heavy dose of educational psychology. Thus one finds chapters on "Left Brain/Right Brain," "The Art of Imaging," and "Holistic Learning." Nevertheless, the "wedge" (a renamed snowplow) is still fundamental to the ATM, and the stem still appears as an intermediate-level turn. Hannes Schneider shouldn't despair.

Friedl Pfeifer and Fred Iselin, co-directors of the Aspen Ski School, catching some air at Aspen, 1953.
NA

Ski schools proliferated all over the country after World War II when many instructors returned from military service. These beginning skiers are lining up for instruction (top) and practicing their snowplow turns at Big Bromley Ski Area, Vt., in March 1947.
USFS

Ernie Blake, ski school director and chief developer of Taos Ski Valley, N.M., teaches his class the kickturn, December 1960. USFS

United States Eastern Amateur Ski Association

EASTERN DIVISION OF THE NATIONAL SKI ASSOCIATION OF AMERICA, INC.

This is to Certify that

Mr. *Robert Billings*

of the *Brattleboro Outing* Club

has qualified as an Amateur Ski Instructor at the
U. S. Eastern Amateur Ski Association's School.

Certificate No. *3*

February 19*35*

President, U.S.E.A.S.A.

Examiner, U.S.E.A.S.A.

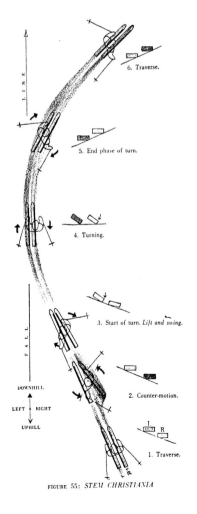

FIGURE 55: *STEM CHRISTIANIA*

6. Traverse.

5. End phase of turn.

4. Turning.

3. Start of turn. *Lift and swing.*

2. Counter-motion.

1. Traverse.

LINE

FALL

DOWNHILL

LEFT RIGHT

UPHILL

I R

Downhill skiing in the early 1900s.

CHAPTER FOUR

GOING FOR GOLD

SKI COMPETITION

Alf Engen, both a top jumper and a racer, takes a gate at the 1947 National Downhill Championships, Alta, Utah.   Utah Historical Society

The origins of downhill racing are almost as obscure as the origins of the sport of skiing. Perhaps the first downhill race took place centuries ago in Scandinavia when a group of soldiers on cross-country skis challenged each other to a run down a snow-covered knoll.

Whatever the case, America's first well-known downhill races were held by that notorious and fun-loving bunch of California gold-panning skiers. Never a modest lot, the miners claimed that their races were the "first organized ski competition the world has ever known."

The Californians made use of racing innovations that, in a more refined form, are in existence to this day—among them a low crouch to minimize wind resistance and the application of downhill wax, or "dope" as they called it, brewed of items like bees' wax and spruce oil. No doubt, too, the miners set the world's speed-skiing record for the era—Tommy Todd's 1879 run down Lost Sierra Mountain where, over a 1,804-foot course, he was clocked at 88 miles per hour.

But the California racing craze was a flash in the pan, so to speak, and by about 1900, when the gold had run out, interest in skiing had largely died with the mining camps. Downhill racing would be reintroduced to America, years later, by way of the Alps.

In the 1870s, ski carnivals became increasingly popular in the Scandinavian countries, but organized competition at these events centered on jumping and cross-country. At about the same time, jumping competitions were being held in Michigan, Minnesota, Wisconsin, and other locales that boasted strong Scandinavian populations and long, hard winters.

As the 19th century drew to a close, skiing caught on in the Alps. With the Alps' steep and open terrain, downhill running, as opposed to jumping and cross-country, naturally became a greater component of skiing; it wasn't long, of course, before the sport's more able practitioners were challenging each other to downhill races.

These early races were casual affairs. As former racer John Tobin writes in his book *The Fall Line,* "The primitive downhill race of 1925 was perhaps the purest ever run. There was simply a mountain to be skied. There were no rules, no prescribed route, and few officials."

The races featured what was known as a "geschmozzel" start. The competitors simply lined up together on top of the mountain, and, with the starter's signal, all bolted off at once, which presented the hazard of a mass pileup once the terrain narrowed. The first to the bottom was declared the winner, with times in the neighborhood of nine minutes for a two-mile course and the runner-up several minutes behind. The racers, including the winners, fell frequently, and sometimes intentionally—the "planned sitzmark" was one way to control speed and direction during an era when downhill technique was in its infancy.

In these early days of downhill racing, before the advent of a predetermined path down the mountain, "choosing a line" was an entirely different matter than it is today. One former European racer tells of getting hung up on a clothesline while trying to take a shortcut through the backyard of a farmhouse. Another racer of the early era, Swiss-born Fred Iselin, who was later director of ski schools at Aspen, recalled a race conducted during a blizzard in the 1930s at Davos, Switzerland. Iselin's anecdote is laden with the flavor of early racing.

Used by Sierra gold miners in the 19th century, these boards were not much for turning; they did, however, offer their passengers speeds approaching 90 miles per hour. This photo was taken in 1949 when a group of skiers reenacted the Sierra racing days of the 1850s, the first competitive ski events in this country.   FH

Iselin didn't know the huge mountain very well, he said in an interview for John Jay's book *Ski Down the Years,* and he couldn't see through the blowing snow, so he decided to follow the racer ahead of him and just make it down the mountain the eight miles to the finish at Kublis. Iselin followed the racer to a saddle partway down the mountain, and at this point his leader turned to the right.

"I go after him," Iselin said, "and suddenly the guy vanishes. And people holler like mad. 'Go left, go left.' There was hundreds of people there on that saddle. And I went left. I had to run a little bit to get over the ridge. And this guy went to [the village of] Klosters. He missed completely. He came down and he went to Klosters, I think, or Wolfgang. And there were about fifteen guys in that race who ended up in Wolfgang instead of Kublis, which was a completely different direction, you know. That was the worst race I ever saw."

If the race courses of the era were rudimentary, so was the equipment, and racers were constantly experimenting with ways to improve it. For instance, Walter Prager, another Swiss who was one of the world's top racers in the early 1930s and who later in the decade coached the powerhouse Dartmouth ski teams, once fixed windshield wipers to his goggles and hooked the blades to an elastic band running underneath his chin. He powered the wipers by opening and closing his mouth. Prager also experimented with one bronze ski edge and one steel edge; the bronze is faster on wet snow, he said, because it's "greasy." Prager used this innovation at one of the Parsenn competitions at Davos, during a race when a man named Rominger was literally right on his heels. On a long traverse, with Rominger right behind, Prager edged his skis very carefully. He told an interviewer for *Ski Down the Years* what happened next:

"I suddenly was pulling away from Rominger . . . and this Rominger shouted, 'What the hell are you doing?' . . . so I just went faster and pulled away further and I won the race by over one whole minute! . . . Yah, those bronze edges slid better on the vet schnow . . . that was the thing! And Rominger vent right out of his mind!"

These early, wild days of ski racing began to change with the introduction of the double-pole racing course. It put a little more predictability—not to mention control—into skiing competition.

The first slalom course had been set in 1905 at Lilienfeld, Austria, by ski pioneer Mathias Zdarsky, but Zdarsky's was a single-pole course, where skiers simply wound around from one pole to the next. Not until 1921, at Murren, Switzerland, did Britain's Arnold Lunn (the British were very good at the early

SIR ARNOLD LUNN. Considered the father of modern ski racing, Lunn, a British subject, invented the double-pole slalom course in the 1920s. Previous to Lunn's invention racers wound from one single pole to the other, or, lacking any course at all, chose their own way down the mountain. Lunn was born in India in 1888 but spent the greater part of his life in the Alps, first skiing at age 10. He was instrumental in organizing some of the world's first big ski races, among them the Arlberg-Kandahar and the first World Alpine Championships. He also helped establish the first U.S. women's ski team and introduce Alpine events to the Olympics. He wrote over 50 books, including several on skiing and mountaineering. In 1952, he was knighted for his contributions to skiing.   NSM downhills) set the first modern slalom using two-gate combinations. Lunn, who was later knighted for his contributions to skiing, was seeking a way to put turning technique (as opposed to a straight schuss) into racing. His double-pole courses, which are still the standard in international competition, required racers to pass through "gates" consisting of two poles each.

Lunn's inventiveness gave birth to slalom competition, an event that was included at the first running of the famed Arlberg-Kandahar in 1928. The first A-K spawned other races in Europe, thus firmly establishing slalom and downhill as legitimate skiing contests. In 1930 the FIS (Federation Internationale de Ski), which until then had been solely concerned with Nordic competition, formally recognized these Alpine events. It wasn't until 1936, however, that downhill and slalom found a place in the Winter Olympics.

Back in the United States, early ski racing was largely the province of college outing clubs. As in Europe, U.S. ski competition until the early 1900s consisted largely of jumping and cross-country. In 1909, however, Fred Harris, a student at Dartmouth College in Hanover, N.H., proposed that undergraduates form an outing club to take advantage of the long New Hampshire winters. Other college outing clubs sprang up throughout the East, and they began to hold ski competitions. Dartmouth skiers would essentially dominate the U.S. racing circuit until World War II.

The early collegiate competition focused on Nordic events, but in 1923 America's first double-pole slalom course was set by Dartmouth Professor Charles Proctor in a competition with Canada's McGill University. In 1927, the first modern downhill in the U.S., the Dartmouth Ski Championship, was held on the Carriage Road at Mount Moosilauke, N.H. The 2.8-mile course dropped 2,800 feet on a switchbacking trail that was, according to one account, "no wider than a cart at any one point." To get a feel for early ski racing in America, one only need note that the first National Downhill Championship was held on this trail in 1933.

The early downhill races were run on primitive courses. Finish of America's first modern downhill race, Mount Moosilauke, N.H., 1927. This was before the days of wide-open trails cut through the timber. **NESM**

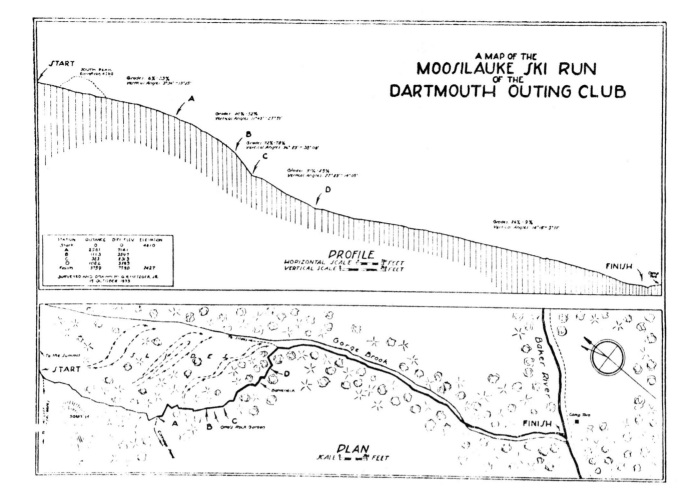

An early Dartmouth ski poster.   WASM

Jumpers at Big Pines, Calif., in 1935. From left: Hjalmar Hvam, who would go on to invent one of the world's first safety bindings and who won three gold medals at the 1932 nationals; Rolf Wigaard; Roy Mikkelsen, 1933 and 1935 national jumping champion. The three jumpers on the right are identified only as Johnny, Jim and Norge.
WASM

Denver Ski Club members at Hot Sulphur Springs, Colo., 1927.   DPL

Jumpers at a Colorado meet, 1920s.
DPL

Elsewhere in America, too, racing caught on during the 1930s. For example, skiers in the West held a counterpart to the Inferno, the Silver Skis race, first run in 1934 on Washington's 14,410-foot Mount Rainier, second highest mountain in the continental United States. Starting at Camp Muir at 10,000 feet, the course dropped 4,600 vertical feet to Paradise Valley. The race originally used a geschmozzel start, had no control gates, and prompted no lack of stories and mishaps—for example, in one running a racer broke his jaw in a collision with another skier, and in another the two top racers were still running neck and neck all the way down at the finish. Meanwhile, California skiers, taking their cue from accounts of the gold miners' races, in 1940 established the Silver Belt race, where the prize, as in the old Sierra races, was a belt studded with silver.

Despite a growing interest in racing, American skiers, for the most part, were no match for the Europeans. The first great American racers, according to some accounts, were Clarita Heath, Marion McKean and Dick Durrance. In the late 1930s, Heath and McKean regularly were placing in the top 10 in the big European races, while Durrance, who learned to ski when spending part of his youth in Germany, placed 10th in the combined at the 1936 Olympics, the first Olympics that included Alpine events.

Durrance skied for Dartmouth during the era when that team, under the guidance of Walter Prager, dominated U.S. collegiate competition, and he later won Sun Valley's prestigious Harriman Cup downhill three times, beating many of his former Olympic rivals.

One of Durrance's better-known racing feats was his thundering third Harriman victory run when he clipped a few spruce trees coming off a steep headwall at about 60 mph. Spectators said he shouted to himself, "You lucky son-uvabitch" as he made it into the clear, and Averell Harriman, in presenting the cup, commented on the blazing run: "Congratulations, Dick—but don't you ever dare do that again!"

Dick Durrance, America's top racer during the 1930s, at Sun Valley, 1939.　　　NSM

Durrance at the 1936 Olympics in Garmisch.
Author's collection

Durrance with Averell Harriman, Sun Valley, 1940. He had just won Sun Valley's Harriman Cup race—one of the premier events on the American racing circuit—for the third time. The race was discontinued in 1965.　　　NESM

SIGRID STROMSTAD LAMING. In 1932, for the first time, women were permitted to enter the National Ski Association championships, held that year at Lake Tahoe. Laming won the cross-country race, the only women's event offered, thus becoming the first national women's ski champion. A native of Norway and a member of California's Auburn Ski Club, she was also an excellent jumper, with a recorded leap of 32 meters.   WASM

A 1929 gelandesprung by Robert O. Baumrucker. A year earlier, Baumrucker, a Dartmouth student, had won the world's first slalom held under rules set down by the FIS and the first slalom in which time alone determined the winner. The race took place March 9, 1928, in Hanover, N.H., and the course was set by Dartmouth Professor Charles A. Proctor, who five years earlier had introduced slalom to the United States. Even in 1928, however, slalom was still so new that, until he entered the race, Baumrucker had never seen a slalom course. Currently he is a resident of San Francisco and maintains an avid interest in ski history.
Robert Baumrucker

The 1930s, a decade when skiing really got a foothold in the United States, also witnessed one of the most spectacular ski races ever held in this country—the legendary American Inferno. The course started on the 6,288-foot summit of New Hampshire's Mount Washington, the highest mountain in New England and site of some of the world's worst weather, and dropped 4,300 vertical feet over four miles to the mountain's base. The highlight of the descent (at least to a spectator) was the plunge down the Headwall at Tuckerman's Ravine, a 1,000-foot-high treeless glacial cirque with a pitch in places steeper than 50 degrees. The racers could take the Headwall in any manner they chose, for the Inferno used no control gates.

It was at the 1939 running of the Inferno that Toni Matt, a young Austrian downhiller, performed his now-legendary schuss. Most racers would make a high-speed traverse across the gentle snowfields on top of Mount Washington, and, as they approached the dropoff into the ravine, they would throw in a few check turns, making a traverse and a few more check turns on the way down the frighteningly steep face.

Not Matt. Matt has said that he planned to make the check turns, but when he got to the lip, he didn't see any sense in turning—it was so steep, a turn wouldn't slow him down anyway. Equipped with 225-cm-long wooden skis, beartrap bindings, and baggy wool pants, he made the upper traverse, turned toward the entrance to the ravine, and dove over the lip, plunging straight down the 1,000-foot drop. He roared past some 2,000 spectators watching from the bottom of the ravine, his skis slapping across the rippled snow, and flew on down the trail to win the race in 6:29, a full minute ahead of Dartmouth's Dick Durrance, who placed second.

Matt was once asked if there was any luck involved in making that schuss. He replied, "You're lucky when you're 19, stupid and have strong legs."

Toni Matt, displaying a very modern-looking racing style, North Conway, N.H., 1946.   NESM

A 1937 view of Tuckerman's Ravine, taken during the running of a downhill race. In the background, spectators line the top of the Little Headwall, while above them looms the face of the main Headwall. Note the racer at the foot of the Little Headwall and the narrowness of the course.   USFS

Matt at Sun Valley. Matt arrived in the United States in 1938 and quickly became one of the leading U.S. ski racers. He was national downhill champion in 1939 and national downhill and combined champion in 1941. He was a member of 10th Mountain Division and has directed several ski schools as well as served as executive director of the Northern Rocky Mountain Ski Association. Despite these achievements, Matt is perhaps best known for his 1939 schuss down the massive Headwall at Tuckerman's Ravine, on New Hampshire's Mount Washington.   WASM

Spectators on Tuckerman's Little Headwall watch a racer negotiate a turn at the headwall's foot, 1937. Tuckerman's Ravine was the site of the famed American Inferno downhill race.   USFS

Tuckerman's Ravine on Mount Washington, showing the Boott Spur slopes, circa 1940. Tuckerman's was, and still is, a popular spot for spring skiing. It is not serviced by ski lifts.   USFS

Eventually, Western universities began to put together some powerful ski teams. Pictured here is the 1942 University of Nevada ski team, champions of the Pacific Coast Intercollegiate Conference. Front from left: Warren Hart, Bob Hirschkind, Back from left: Ashley Van Slyck, Barnes Berry, Duane Ramsey, Bill Bechdolt, Bill Nelson and Jerry Wetzel.   WASM

Interscholastic ski team members, Windham, Vt., 1930.   NESM

The Dartmouth ski team when it was very young, date unknown. In the 1930s, Dartmouth skiers essentially dominated U.S. Alpine ski competition.   CSM

The finish line of a 1941 race at the Arizona Snow Bowl. Operating a Forest Service radio is Ranger Harold Pilmer, surrounded by judges and timing officials. Radios were used to communicate between starting gate and finish line, as well as to monitor conditions along the course. The radios also were used during the summer for forest fire communications; ski races gave forest officials the opportunity for year-round practice.   USFS

Running gates at Mount Rose Ski Area, Nev. Note the tree branch used as a slalom pole; today's slalom poles are spring-loaded plastic tubes that automatically snap upright when knocked over.   FH

Olympic tryouts at Snoqualmie Pass, Wash., held under the auspices of the Seattle Ski Club and the National Ski Association. Date unknown; judging from the outfits this was probably the late 1920s or early 30s.
State Historical Society of Wisconsin

Denver University ski team on the way East to race Dartmouth, 1940s. In the 1950s, Denver's ski team replaced Dartmouth as the dominant force in college racing. Olympic skier Gordon Wren is in the center, wearing a hat.   CSM

The United States ski team fielded for the 1940 Olympics, according to some observers, would have given the Europeans plenty of competition, but the war intervened, and many of the top American skiers joined the ski troops. International competition ceased from 1940 to 1947; the first FIS World Championships after the war would be held in 1950 at Aspen, then a struggling new resort eager for publicity.

After the war, the American women racers captured the limelight. In 1948, Gretchen Fraser became the first American to win an Olympic medal when she took the gold in slalom and the silver in Alpine combined at St. Moritz. Four years later, at the Oslo Olympics, American skier Andrea Mead Lawrence captured two golds—one in slalom and one in giant slalom—and found a place on the cover of *Time* magazine. Oslo was the first time giant slalom had been held as a separate Olympic event—it had been developed just before the war as a sort of compromise between the speed of downhill and the tight, acrobatic turns of slalom.

American hopes for a men's Olympic medal began to look good when Buddy Werner, of Steamboat Springs, Colo., appeared on the racing scene. At age 17, Werner outskied a world-class field to win the 1954 Holmenkollen downhill. While he put in strong performances throughout the 1950s, his entire career was plagued by bad luck and he was frequently taken out of the competition by falls and injuries. He was world downhill champion in 1959, and was unofficially acknowledged as the world's best skier, but he had no chance to prove it as an ankle fracture sidelined him for the 1960 Olympics in Squaw Valley. In those games, American Penny Pitou picked up silvers in the giant slalom and downhill while Betsy Snite took second in the slalom and Tom Corcoran placed fourth in the giant slalom.

After the '60 Olympics, Werner increasingly gave himself to helping younger racers, and he never did claim an Olympic medal. In the 1964 games at Innsbruck, his younger teammates, Billy Kidd and Jimmy Heuga, took second and third, respectively, in the slalom, becoming the first American male Alpine skiers to win Olympic medals. Werner, tragically, died in an avalanche soon after his retirement from racing in 1964.

Not until the 1984 Winter Olympics at Sarajevo—48 years after the U.S. first sent an Alpine team to the Olympics—did an American male, downhiller Bill Johnson, capture an Olympic gold, a performance repeated shortly thereafter by Phil Mahre, who won the slalom with brother Steve taking second.

In the last few decades, ski racing has undergone numerous developments and offshoots. Professional racing got underway in the 1960s, and racers fought head-to-head down dual slalom courses in a bid for prize money. "Speed skiing," though not a new development, has been growing in popularity, its participants wearing streamlined outfits that look like they were borrowed from a visiting alien and reaching speeds of well over 100 miles per hour down long,

Andrea Mead, age 14, racing at Sun Valley, March 1947.   NA

NESM

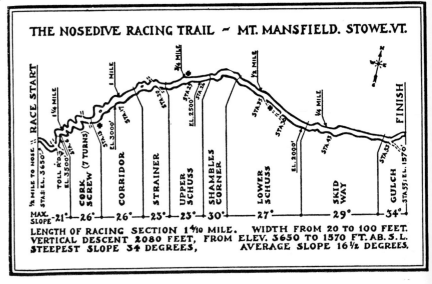

-48-

Gretchen Fraser, winner of America's first medal in Olympic Alpine skiing.   NSM

Top-notch husband and wife racing team. Gretchen Kunigke Fraser, gold-medal winner in the 1948 Olympics, and husband Don, U.S. Olympic team member, swoop down Galena Summit, near Sun Valley, Idaho.   NESM

Observers from the Russian Ski Federation flank George H. Watson, "mayor" of Alta, Utah, during the 1950 FIS races at Aspen, Colo. These races put Aspen on the map.
    FH

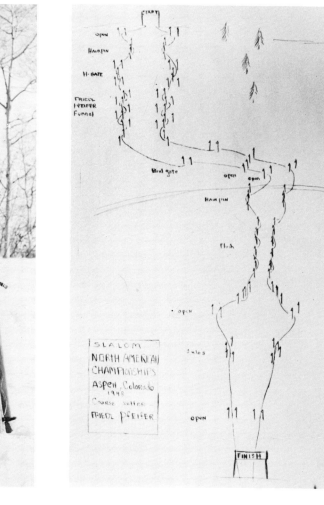

NESM

Andrea Mead blasts down a course in the 1950 Harriman Cup races; two years later this form and this aggressiveness would win her two gold medals at the Winter Olympics.   WASM

Othmar Schneider of Lech, Austria, races at Mount Mansfield, Vt., while Olympic champion Andrea Mead Lawrence watches, 1953.   NA

straight, extremely steep courses. Another development has been the World Cup, started in 1966 as a championship series for the world's best racers, while for the recreational skier there is NASTAR, modeled in part after the citizens' races of Europe, but permitting skiers to compare their times against a nation-wide standard.

With NASTAR and with scores of junior racing programs now organized throughout the nation, American ski racing, once exclusively the province of "daredevil" gold miners and then of college students out for a little wintertime fun, has finally come to the masses.

Bob Beattie, coach of the U.S. ski team through much of the 1960s. Racers on his 1964 Olympic team won four medals at Innsbruck; later he helped develop the professional racing circuit and the NASTAR racing program.

NASTAR

The NASTAR program has opened up ski racing to the casual recreational skier. Over one million skiers have participated in NASTAR races all across the country since the program was developed by SKI magazine in 1968. Under NASTAR's handicap system, racers are able to compare their abilities with participants elsewhere in the country. NASTAR

University of Denver freshman Buddy Werner, of Steamboat Springs, Colo., gets a kiss from his sister, Gladys, in March 1955 after winning the Intercollegiate Downhill Ski Race on Stowe's Nose Dive Trail. Werner would go on to become one of the world's top ski racers in the late 1950s. He was killed in an avalanche in 1964.   NA

Jimmy Heuga, future Olympic bronze medal winner, racing at Sugar Bowl in 1954. Age 11.   WASM

WILLY SCHAEFFLER. The Vince Lombardi of skiing, Schaeffler is known for his tough coaching and his championship ski teams. He has been active in many facets of skiing. He was born in Germany in 1916 and forced into the German army in World War II. After the war he served as ski instructor for the U.S. Army in Germany, immigrating to this country in 1948. He was coach of the Denver University ski team from 1948 to 1970; during that time his teams won 14 NCAA championships. He was coach of the 1966, 1968 and 1970 FISU teams, served as director of ski events for the 1960 Winter Olympics at Squaw Valley, and was program director for the USSA Alpine teams from 1971-73. He helped found the Professional Ski Instructors of America (PSIA) and helped build Colorado's Arapahoe Ski Basin, also serving as its ski school director.   NESM

DICK "MAD DOG" BUEK. "Dick Buek," it is said, "knew only one pace—all out." A top downhiller in the early 1950s, Buek grew up on Donner Summit, Calif. He didn't start skiing until he was 17, but, after coaching from Hannes Schroll of nearby Sugar Bowl, Buek won the National Downhill championships in 1952 and 1954. Buek was a daredevil in every sport he pursued, and his feats have become legend. He schussed Sun Valley's Exhibition the first time he saw it; he dove off the cliffs of Acapulco to win gas money for the trip home; he won a meet during his first attempt at ski jumping; he piloted a small plane through a "slalom" course formed by Squaw Valley's lift towers, flying under the cables. In addition to his national downhill titles, Buek placed 12th, despite a fall, in the downhill at the 1952 Olympics. He died in 1957 when his plane crashed into Donner Lake.   WASM

Alex Bright—racer, Olympian, and backer of the Cannon Mountain aerial tram. On the Taft Trail at Cannon Mountain.
NESM

Summer racing camp at Bachelor Butte, near Bend, Ore., 1966. In the past 20 years many summer racing camps have been established in the Western states, often placing portable lifts high on the snowfields above timberlines.
Author's collection

SKI JUMPING

Ski jumping is a Nordic event; technically speaking, it does not fall within the scope of this book. Yet, at one point, ski jumping played a very significant role in the development of American downhill skiing. In the late 19th and early 20th centuries, jumpers were on the cutting edge of the American ski scene, and their meets, which could draw up to 15,000 non-skiing spectators, were essentially the nation's only organized ski events. Likewise, it was the jumpers who organized America's first nationwide ski association, an association that eventually gave its blessing to Alpine ski competition. In the early years of this century, however, downhill skiers were few, and jumpers were the dominant force in American skiing.

A surprising number of jumping photographs survive from this era; following is a sampling of them.

HARPERS WEEKLY of March 12, 1892, ran this drawing entitled "Norwegian Sport at Ishpeming, Michigan."

Michigan State Archives

As far away as Alaska, skiers were riding the jumping hills in the early 20th century. An improvised ski jump in Nome, Alaska, 1906, and a ski jumper who looks like he's heading for a rough landing.

Alaska Historical Library

While many of the early jumpers were Scandinavian by birth, the flag of their adopted country was much in evidence at their jumping meets. Hot Sulphur Springs, Colo.

CHS

During the early years of this century, Steamboat Springs, Colo., was a hotbed of jumping. The tradition still lives at Steamboat's two jumps at Howelsen Hill, named after Carl Howelsen, who did much to introduce skiing to Colorado.　　　　CHS

Jumping hill near the University of Utah in Salt Lake City, 1922.   CHS

Jumping meets were festive occasions. Ski jump at Genessee Mountain, near Denver, Colo. 1920.   DPL

Snow had to be hauled in to cover the outrun of this jump at Idaho Springs, Colo., just west of Denver, 1920.   DPL

Roy Mikkelsen, one of America's greatest ski jumpers. Norwegian by birth, he came to the United States in 1924. In 1933 he won his first National Ski Jumping Championship and repeated the feat in 1935. Mikkelsen was the Auburn Ski Club's leading jumper and was a member of the 1936 Olympic team. During World War II he was a member of the 10th Mountain Division and the 99th Norwegian American Battalion. He died in 1967.   WASM

Constructing the ski jump at Franconia, N.H., 1930s.
NESM

Flying high over a ski jump in Utah. The jumper on the left appears to be holding a bouquet of flowers in his hand.
FH

Carl Howelsen, "The Flying Norseman," was already a top jumper and cross-country skier in his native Norway when he emigrated to the United States in 1905. He became a performer with the Barnum and Bailey Circus, which showcased his jumping skills, and he helped organize the Norge Ski Club in Chicago. In 1910 he moved west to Colorado and helped establish jumping hills and competition in Hot Sulphur Springs and Steamboat Springs. He is sometimes called "the father of Colorado skiing." In 1921 he won the National Professional Ski Championships at Genessee Mountain and a year later returned to Norway to visit his parents, never again to see the Colorado mountains. He married and settled down in Norway, but continued to jump until he was 71 years old. He died in 1955.   NSM

"Carl Howelson" Record 171 Feet Steamboat Springs Ski Carnival -March 1-2-1917- -8- -Out West Photo- Boulder-

Howelsen performed throughout the country for the Barnum and Bailey Circus in the early 1900s. Note the arrows indicating his direction of flight, apparently for the benefit of those who had never heard of this strange sport.   Circus World Museum, Baraboo, Wis.

The large ski-jump complex at Berlin, N.H.
Author's collection

Lowell Thomas Jr., son of the famous news commentator, wins the ski jump at the 1948 Dartmouth Winter Carnival.   NA

National Jumping Championships at Ishpeming, Feb. 22, 1906. This jumper clearly was not winning many style points.
Michigan State Archives

The Brass Wire Jump at Ishpeming, Mich., 1905. A bastion of ski jumping, Ishpeming was the birthplace of America's first nationwide ski organization. Jumping is still popular in the town.
NESM

Ecker's Hill near Salt Lake City. The larger takeoff ramp was used by professional jumpers, while the smaller one was used by amateurs and during poor weather. The 1932 National Professional Championships were held on this hill.

Utah State Historical Society

South Dakota had no lack of Scandinavian immigrants. Pictured is the Sioux Valley Ski Club jump at Canton, S.D., the site of several national jumping championships. NSM

SCORE CARD

"The Day of a Thousand Thrills"

FINAL
OLYMPIC TRY - OUT

Ski Tournament

Under Supervision of
Olympic Ski Games Committee

CANTON, S. D.

Held under the Auspices of the Sioux Valley Ski Club

Ski jumps were found in some unlikely places. Pictured is a jump at Gary, Ind., 1932. At one point, ski jumping was the only ski sport in the state, but Indiana now boasts at least four ski areas.

Chicago Historical Society

Two of America's premier ski jumpers, Art Devlin (left), of Lake Placid, and Art Tokle (right), of Brooklyn, prepare their skis for a Norge Ski Club meet at Fox River Grove, Ill., 1951.   NA

Flying high over a town in Maine.

Maine State Archives

Minnesota has always had a strong winter sports and ski jumping tradition, thanks in part to its hard winters and its large Scandinavian population. Pictured is the jump at Indian Mounds, in the capital city of St. Paul, 1940. Note the large crowds along the outrun and on the surrounding hills.

Minnesota Historical Society

Pomona, in Southern California, was the site of this 255-foot-high jump, built in 1951 at the Los Angeles County Fair. Six Olympic team members participated in the jump meet. NA

For sheer spectacle, ski jumping has always been a crowd pleaser, a fact that was not lost on meet organizers and promoters. This jump was constructed inside Chicago's Grant Park in 1954.

New York City's Madison Square Garden hosted a jumping meet in the 1930s. For many years, ski shows also were held in the Garden.   Author's collection

Ski jump built at the Utah State Fairgrounds. An ice rink apparently was being constructed alongside.
Utah State Historical Society

A jumper begins his flight over Berkeley, Calif., in 1934. Sponsored by the Auburn Ski Club, this was the first San Francisco Bay Jumping Championship. Snow was brought down from the mountains in railroad cars; over 15,000 spectators attended the meet. Most were gate crashers and the club lost money. Roy Mikkelsen won the meet, which ended when a huge snowball fight broke out among the kids in attendance. Another meet was held the following year.   WASM

The National Jumping Championships were held at the 1939 Golden Gate Exposition on Treasure Island in San Francisco Bay. The jump was 185 feet high and the "snow" was provided by the Union Ice Co. The meet was organized by the Auburn Ski Club, which earlier had held several tournaments in Berkeley.

Left: FH   Right: WASM

SOME NOTABLE AMERICAN SKI JUMPERS

Alf Engen. Engen immigrated to the U.S. from his native Norway. In 1931, at age 22, he won the National Professional Jumping Championships after winning numerous regional titles. Engen won many other jumping titles and downhill races until he retired in 1948. He worked for many years in ski area development throughout the West, including Sun Valley, and as ski school director at Alta, Utah. He is truly one of America's most versatile athletes with numerous awards in skiing, soccer, hockey and ice skating.   NSM

Sverre Engen. Like his brother Alf, Sverre immigrated to the U.S. and became a national jumping champion. For seven winters in the 1930s, he toured the country as a professional ski jumper, introducing the sport to thousands of people. Engen was also a downhill racer, ski area developer, instructor, avalanche control expert and producer of ski movies.   NSM

Olav Ulland, Seattle, Wash. Ulland was one of the finest jumpers of his time, and the first in the world to jump over 100 meters. In 1936, he coached the Italian Olympic jumping team and the following year he came to the U.S. as jumping coach for the Seattle Ski Club and Leavenworth Winter Sports Club. He has had a long career in national and international jumping competition and has been active in a successful ski and sporting goods business on the West Coast.
NSM

Gordon Wren, born and raised in Steamboat Springs, Colo., was known as America's best all-around skier. He was the only American ever to qualify for all four events in the Winter Olympics. A member of the 1948 Olympic team, he won a fifth place medal in the special jumping event. During the same season he set jumping hill records in Switzerland at Arosa, St. Moritz, and Davos. He was the first jumper to break the 300-foot mark in America. In 1950, he was a member of the FIS jumping team. That year he was national Nordic combined champion and won a second place in the national giant slalom competition.   FH

John Balfanz, one of America's finest jumpers. During the 1960s he made the FIS team, the 1964 Olympic team and set two North American distance records.   NSM

CHAPTER FIVE

THE GAMES

AMERICA AND THE WINTER OLYMPICS

The Olympic ski jump at Squaw Valley. Set in the trees, it was protected from wind and avalanches. Squaw Valley was the site of the 1960 Winter Olympics, while Lake Placid, N.Y., hosted America's two other Winter Games, in 1932 and 1980.   USFS

More than any single event, the 1932 Winter Olympics at Lake Placid, N.Y., changed the way in which Americans regarded winter. Before the Olympics, winter was looked upon as a time to huddle indoors, away from the snow and cold; even among the outdoorsy set, winter activities largely consisted of getting ready for fishing and baseball seasons.

The 1932 Olympics changed all that. While Alpine skiing was not on the agenda, the Games did feature ski jumping, bobsledding, ice skating, and cross-country skiing. Following these events through newspapers and radio, millions of Americans discovered that there were indeed ways to have fun in the snow.

Likewise, the two other Winter Olympics held in this country—the 1960 Games at Squaw Valley, Calif., and the 1980 Games, again at Lake Placid—exposed many more Americans to the wintertime outdoors. The 1960 and 1980 games did include Alpine skiing, and, through television, the hard-charging performances of the world's best skiers were flashed into living rooms across the nation. For many viewers, this was an invitation to try a new and exciting sport.

The story of America's first Winter Olympics goes back to the winter of 1904-05 when the Lake Placid Club, a fashionable resort in the little village in upstate New York, took a gamble and decided to stay open for the winter season. Along with sports such as ice skating and tobogganing, the club offered skiing that first season, importing from Norway 40 pairs of skis and 40 single poles.

These 40 pairs established Lake Placid as America's first continuously operating ski and winter sports resort. While other ski resorts were established elsewhere in the nation early this century, Lake Placid remained a leader in the field. As such, in the late 1920s Lake Placid began to look at the possibility of hosting the 1932 Winter Olympics.

Skiers at Lake Placid during the winter of 1904-05. This was the first winter that skiing was offered at the resort, which would be the site of both the 1932 and 1980 Winter Olympics. Lake Placid is America's oldest continuously operating winter sports and ski resort. Far left, Edward C. Dana; seated center, Dr. Edgar VanderVeer; standing rear, Godfrey Dewey (who would be instrumental in bringing the 1932 Games to Lake Placid); second right, Mrs. VanderVeer; far right, Henry Van Hoevenberg.

Mary MacKenzie
Lake Placid, N.Y.

Founders of Lake Placid's Sno Birds, one of America's earliest and most active ski clubs. Left to right: Leslie May, Henry Uihlein, Carl A. Reimer, Hugh Robinson, W.H. Waring, Philip Lowry, Count Ernest Des Baillets. Portrait taken on the Lake Placid Club ice rink, 1921.

Mary MacKenzie
Lake Placid, N.Y.

H. Smith "Jack Rabbit" Johannsen, famous early ski instructor at Lake Placid, pictured with his class on the Lake Placid golf course, early 1920s. Johannsen now lives in Canada. When he was 108 he still skied.

Mary MacKenzie
Lake Placid, N.Y.

Taking the "bumps" on the Lake Placid golf course.

Mary MacKenzie
Lake Placid, N.Y.

Behind it all was the Lake Placid Club's secretary, Dr. Godfrey Dewey, whose father, Melvil, had founded the club as well as the Dewey Decimal System. In 1928, Godfrey Dewey traveled to Europe to see the site of the first Winter Olympics, which had been held in 1924 at Chamonix, France, and went to St. Moritz where he was manager of the U.S. ski team for the 1928 Olympics. Returning to Lake Placid, he spoke before a meeting of the local Kiwanis, the chamber of commerce, and the village board, and managed to sell local officials on the idea, in part by explaining that Lake Placid already had most of the necessary facilities. He then convinced the International Olympic Committee (IOC) of the desirability of Lake Placid, despite bids for the Games from Oslo, Montreal, Minnesota, Colorado, Yosemite, and the California legislature, which offered up to $3 million to help pay for an Olympics held in that state.

Meanwhile, the stock market crashed, but New York state offered $500,000 to host the Games, while other funds came from the local sale of bonds. The Games' budget, which included an ice arena and bobsled run, was about $1 million, a drop in the bucket compared to the $20 million that would be spent at Squaw Valley, the $178 million spent on Lake Placid's 1980 Olympics, and the $700 million the Japanese spent on the 1972 Sapporo Olympics.

The big problem for the 1932 Olympics (aside from some displays of nationalism resulting from growing international tension) was the weather. Not much snow had fallen in Lake Placid since early November, and the area had been hit by unusual warm spells. Shortly before the Games were to open, the ice on the bobsled run had melted, and the ice on Mirror Lake, where some of the events were scheduled, was unfit for skating.

But the people of Lake Placid persevered, finally digging snow off of nearby mountainsides and hauling it to the ski jumps, and the Games went on. They have been described as a "folksy" Olympics, with food served by local women's groups, transportation provided by sleigh, and security handled by a contingent of 53 state troopers.

A total of 80,000 spectators showed up to watch the 400-some competitors from 17 nations, including Norwegian figure skater Sonja Henie. Among those in attendance were Lowell Thomas, New York Mayor Jimmy Walker, and Admiral Richard Byrd, who was looking for recruits for polar exploration.

The Americans did remarkably well in the non-skiing events, taking six gold medals—four in speed skating and two in bobsledding. (Due to the weather, some of the bobsledding events were held a day after the Games officially closed.) But the skiing events were a different story. They were dominated by the Scandinavians, especially by the Norwegians. This was a sign of things to come; it would be many years before Americans could ski on a par with the Europeans.

Godfrey Dewey, the man who brought the Olympics to Lake Placid. NSM

III Olympic Winter Games

Lake Placid, USA
February 4-13 1932

-71-

Opening ceremonies of the III Winter Olympic Games, held at Lake Placid, N.Y., Feb. 4-13, 1932.

Author's collection

60-meter jump at Lake Placid. Birger Ruud, an 18-year-old Norwegian, won the gold medal and Norway captured the top three places in the jumping event at the 1932 Games.

Mary MacKenzie
Lake Placid, N.Y.

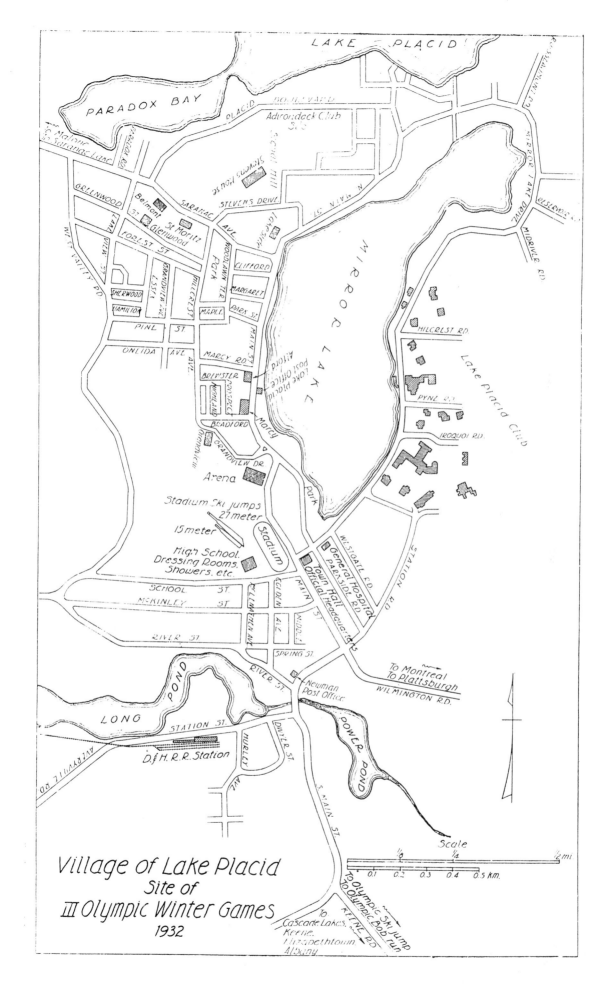

Village of Lake Placid
Site of
III Olympic Winter Games
1932

-73-

Between 1932 and 1960, when America held its next Winter Olympics, great changes were made to the Games. For one thing, they grew greatly in size and popularity; for another, Alpine skiing events—at first only slalom and downhill—were included starting with the 1936 Games at Garmisch-Partenkirchen, Germany, while giant slalom was added in 1952 at Oslo. In 1948 at St. Moritz, 29-year-old Gretchen Fraser won a gold in the slalom, a silver in the combined, and a place in U.S. Alpine skiing history. As the headline for one newspaper dispatch read: "Housewife Wins First U.S. Ski Medal."

Actually, that headline is no longer true. California's Anders Haugen won a bronze in jumping and cross-country combined at the Games in 1924, but due to a scoring error at the time, Haugen's third was only recently discovered. Nevertheless, Fraser's is still the first U.S. Alpine medal, and her performance is still remembered as an impressive feat.

Fraser was a resident of Tacoma, Wash. Her racing career had been interrupted by marriage, a family business, and the war. She was out of practice at the time, but she tried out for the U.S. Olympic team. In addition to becoming popular among the other competitors, she won a berth on the team. In St. Moritz, the pig-tailed Fraser drew number one in the slalom starting order, and was in first place after the first run. As she stood in the starting gate for the second run, the course's communication system broke down, forcing her to wait 18 minutes before taking her run. She kept her concentration, however, and completed a fine run to win the gold, celebrating her victory with a ride back to town in an open sleigh.

Anders Haugen, the first American to win an Olympic medal in skiing, although he waited 50 years to receive it. Haugen immigrated from Norway to the United States in 1909 and became a champion jumper. In 1924, he was named to the U.S. Olympic team and chosen team captain. He made the longest jump during the 1924 Games, but the judges made an error when they computed his points for style and distance. As a result, Haugen was given fourth place. In 1974, the error was discovered, and Haugen was invited to Norway to receive a bronze medal. He died in 1984 at the age of 95.   NSM

Bill Berry, Bob Beattie, and Anders Haugen in Norway, 1974.
NSM

Members of the 1924 Men's U.S. Olympic team, which competed at Chamonix, France. These were the first Winter Olympics, and they did not include Alpine skiing events. Downhill and slalom were added to the Games starting in 1936. From left: Ragnar Omtredt, Harry Lien, George Leach, Anders Haugen, Le Moine Batson.   NESM

Other members of the 1924 team. From left: Anders Haugen, Le Moine Batson, Harry Lien, Sigurd Overbye, John Carleton.   NESM

The 1928 Men's U.S. Olympic team, which competed at St. Moritz, Switzerland. From left: unidentified standard bearer; Anders Haugen; Charles N. Proctor; Rolf Monsen; Godfrey Dewey, manager; G.F. Kirby, representing Gen. Douglas MacArthur, president of the U.S. Olympic Committee.   NESM

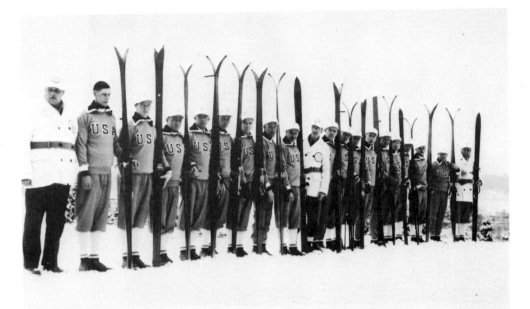

The 1932 U.S. Olympic ski team. Its members competed at Lake Placid, N.Y.   WASM

The 1936 Men's U.S. Olympic team, which competed at Garmisch-Partenkirchen, Germany. From left: Albert Washburn, Alfred D. Lindley, Alexander Bright, George Page, William Crookes, Richard Durrance, Robert Livermore, Jr.   NESM

The 1936 Women's U.S. Olympic team. From left: Lillian Swann, Mary Bird, Ethlynne Smith, Grace Carter, Helen Boughton-Leigh, Clarita Heath, Elizabeth Woolsey, Marian McKean.   NESM

The 1936 men's team posed for pictures on the boat en route to Europe.　　　　　NSM

The 1936 men's team in Germany.
NESM

Dick Durrance on the race course at the Garmisch Olympics, 1936. Note the German troops along the course.　　　　　NESM

Thirty years later (1966) members of the 1936 Women's U.S. Olympic team met for a reunion. From left: Clarita Heath Bright, Grace Lindley McKnight, Helen Boughton-Leigh McAlpine, Betty Woolsey, Marian McKean Wigglesworth, Mary Bird Young.   WASM

The 1952 U.S. Olympic team, which competed at Oslo, Norway. From left: Coach Emile Allais, Bill Beck, Dick Buek, Dave Lawrence, Jack Nagel, Goodwin, Piutey Robison, Brookie Dodge, Jack Reddish, John Herbert, Kaiser, Gretchen Fraser, Andrea Mead Lawrence, Sandy Tomlinson, Catherine Rudolph, Betty Wier, Sally Neidlinger, Janette Burr, (unidentified), Herbert Jochum.   WASM

Members of the 1960 U.S. Olympic team, which competed in the VIII Winter Games at Squaw Valley, Calif. Bottom row: Dave Lawrence, Andrea Mead Lawrence, Charles Little, Bill Beck. Second row: Renie Cox, Beverly Anderson, Linda Meyers, Joan Hannah, Penny Pitou, Betsy Snite. Third row: Gordon Eaton, Dave Gorsuch, Marvin Melville, Max Marolt. Top row: Chuck Ferries, Thomas Corcoran, Frank Brown, Jim Barrier. NESM

A year after Fraser's victory, a small ski area opened high in California's Sierra Mountains—Squaw Valley, the area that was to become host to America's second Winter Olympics.

An airline pilot by the name of Wayne E. Poulsen was the man who saw Squaw Valley's potential as a ski area. Poulsen had initially visited the then-undeveloped valley in 1932 on a fishing trip and made frequent visits thereafter. An avid skier, he organized and competed on the University of Nevada ski team and for a time taught at Sun Valley, but in 1942 he returned to Squaw Valley, settling there with his bride, Sandy. (It was Sandy Poulsen who gave KT-22, one of Squaw's ski mountains, its name—it took her 22 kickturns to negotiate its face.)

When the Poulsens first lived there, Squaw Valley was little more than a marshy meadow surrounded by beautiful skiable mountains. They had to make do without electricity, running water, or winter access. Yet Poulsen had the dream of building a ski area.

In 1943 and again in 1948, Poulsen purchased property until he owned the entire valley floor, then found the backing to develop it when, on a ski trip to Alta, he met Alexander Cushing, a socially prominent, Harvard-educated New York lawyer. Cushing visited the valley, and, along with the Poulsens and other backers, formed the Squaw Valley Development Corp., with Wayne Poulsen as its president.

Alexander Cushing, the inspiration behind the 1960 Winter Olympics at Squaw Valley. WASM

Squaw Valley, before it was a ski area. The valley's name was given by pioneers in the mid-19th century, who arrived to find primarily children and squaws camped in the area, as the men were away on a journey. It became a high-mountain farming community, but then its population dwindled. It was developed as a ski area in the late 1940s.
WASM

A 1929 movie, THE COVERED WAGON, was filmed at Squaw Valley.
WASM/Carson White

But conflicts over how to develop the area arose between Cushing and Poulsen. With Cushing and his backers holding majority interest, Poulsen was soon out of the corporation. Poulsen retained ownership of most of the valley floor, while the corporation held six acres at the valley's head, where the Forest Service had allotted ski lift permits.

Despite the conflicts, Squaw Valley opened on Thanksgiving 1949 with one double chair, two rope tows and accommodations for 50 guests. The early years were sometimes rough—the valley floor flooded occasionally (the lift operators once showed up at the lodge for lunch in a canoe), and the heavy Sierra snowfalls brought lift-smashing avalanches. But the valley soon gained a reputation for its fine skiing. Adding to its reputation was Emile Allais, who headed the ski school, and Hollywood celebrities, who began stopping by on their way to Sun Valley.

Squaw Valley was still a small resort when, in 1954, Alexander Cushing announced that Squaw would bid for the 1960 Olympics. It wasn't so much that Cushing wanted the Olympics—what he really wanted was publicity for the resort. "I had no more interest in getting the Games than the man in the moon," he once told a reporter for *Time* magazine. "It was just a way of getting some newspaper space."

But the idea of an Olympics at Squaw picked up support. Jo Marillac, a prominent French mountaineer who was then heading Squaw's ski school, reassured Cushing that he "had the mountain, had the snow, and could build the rest." The citizens of California also liked the idea, and the state legislature approved $1 million if Squaw got the Games. Still, the IOC had to be sold on Squaw; to do so, Squaw enlisted the help of George Weller, a former classmate of Cushing's at Harvard and a reporter for the Chicago *Daily News*.

After visiting the valley and seeing how lacking it was in facilities to hold an event the magnitude of the Olympics, Weller came up with the angle that Cushing would use with the IOC: Squaw Valley, as a simple mountain resort, was a place where the Olympic ideals could flourish. (It is said that Weller also had the brochures promoting Squaw printed in English, French and Spanish, but not German, a move that scored points with the Latin American delegation.)

Closing ceremonies of the 1960 Olympics at Squaw Valley. The opening and closing ceremonies were orchestrated by Walt Disney. The Olympic flag shown here was furled and prepared for shipment to Rome, where it would fly over the Summer Games.   USFS

Squaw Peak, site of the men's downhill, is in the center; KT-22 is on the left.

The women's giant slalom began high above the base area on KT-22. USFS

Travelling to Paris to meet with the IOC and vie with the other hopeful sites, Cushing brought along a scale model of Squaw Valley. The model, it turned out, was too large to fit through the IOC's doors, and it had to be set up in a building down the street. Escorting the delegates to see the model gave Squaw's promoters invaluable extra time to sell their product.

In the end, after an effective speech by Cushing and a lot of shouting and floor stamping by those in attendance, the IOC presented the Games to Squaw on the second ballot by a vote of 32 to 30.

A committee was organized to get the Games going, headed by Prentis Hale, a prominent California businessman. Hale was faced with the task of raising some big money—$3.5 million was needed for an ice arena, $1.8 million for an Olympic Village, and almost $1 million for water and sewage, not to mention roads, lifts, and other amenities. Squaw was spared the major expense of building a bobsled run, as the IOC eliminated the event for the 1960 Games, but the total cost eventually came to almost $20 million. To raise it, Hale and colleagues lobbied the California legislature, which gave nearly $8 million, while the U.S. Congress gave $4 million and U.S. companies such as IBM and Disney (which staged the opening and closing ceremonies free of charge) gave help and equipment.

Between 1955, when Squaw got the Olympics, and the opening of the Games in 1960, there was no lack of squabbling and bad press, but construction proceeded. In 1959, Squaw staged the North American Games as a sort of test run for the Olympics—and a test it was. Shortly before the North Americans opened, Squaw got five feet of snow, then rain, then another four feet of snow. The avalanche control teams and foot packers worked frantically, but finally the courses had to be moved to parts of the valley where the snowfall had been brought under control.

A year later, on Feb. 18, 1960, the VIII Winter Olympics opened at Squaw Valley. Again, it had snowed several days prior to the opening, but just as ceremonies commenced the sun came out. Doves were released and Andrea Mead Lawrence, winner of two golds in the 1952 Olympics, skied down the mountain with the Olympic torch.

Aerial view of most of the Olympic facilities at Squaw Valley. Top, left to right: Olympic Village; bus parking zone. Middle, left to right: Squaw Valley Inn; Olympic press building; administrative building; IBM computing center; ice arena. Lower middle, left to right: spectator center; figure skating rink; speed skating oval.   USFS

The Olympic ski jump at Squaw Valley. The 1960 Olympics were characterized by good weather and a holiday atmosphere. Note the airborne ski jumper and his long shadow.
USFS

The Games generally were regarded as one of the best ever. Part of the reason was the intimacy of the little valley, where all but the Nordic events were held and where 22,000 spectators gathered each day. The weather was good, a holiday spirit prevailed, and the 700 athletes from 30 nations competed against each other on mountainsides and ice rinks by day, and by night gathered for parties and dances where they were entertained by Hollywood stars and big-name bands.

In the Alpine skiing events, Americans Penny Pitou and Betsy Snite earned the nickname the "Silver Queens"—Pitou for second places in downhill and giant slalom, Snite for a silver in the slalom. Tom Corcoran was the top American male skier with a fourth in giant slalom, while on the ice rink, the U.S. hockey team triumphed for a gold.

With the 1960 Games, Squaw Valley's reputation was secured. The resort grew dramatically in the following years, eventually sprawling across five mountains and boasting one of the world's largest networks of lifts.

Main Street of Lake Placid, 1951. The village continued to be a popular winter sports resort after the 1932 Olympics, although it was slow in developing major downhill skiing facilities.   NA

In the late 1950s, work was completed on the Whiteface Mountain Ski Center, which would become the site for all the Alpine events during the 1980 Winter Olympics.

Nancie Battaglia
Lake Placid, N.Y.

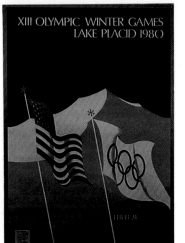

Twenty years after the pageantry at Squaw Valley, America hosted its third Winter Olympics, returning to the site of the 1932 Games at Lake Placid. In the years after the '32 Olympics, the winter sports complex at Lake Placid, as at Squaw Valley, had grown considerably. Lake Placid boasted some 250 miles of cross-country ski trails, a 60-meter jump, and other facilities. But, curiously, the development of its downhill ski areas came quite slowly.

There were several reasons for this. First, Lake Placid strove against a natural handicap of heavily wooded terrain, lacking treeless slopes for open skiing. More significantly, it was hemmed in by the New York state forest preserve which, according to law, "shall forever be wild forest land." Not a tree could be cut without a constitutional amendment approved by the voters. It would be some years before the problems were overcome and a major ski center was constructed on state land.

Insert: Gov. Averell Harriman at Lake Placid. He was the founder of Sun Valley as well as a driving force behind the construction of the Whiteface ski area.
Lake Placid Chamber of Commerce

Meanwhile, in the rope tow and ski train era of the 1930s, the community did what was possible with available private lands. A few small ski centers sprang up in or near the village. In 1938 a larger center, Scott's Cobble, with a vertical drop of 500 feet, was opened. This was a system of open slopes and downhill trails designed by Otto Schniebs with a rope tow installed by Fred Pabst's Ski Tow Inc., eventually replaced by a Poma lift. Two other larger centers, Fawn Ridge and Mount Whitney, followed, and all three became enormously popular. Scott's persisted until 1973, Fawn Ridge until 1977, and Whitney is still in existence.

A half dozen downhill and racing trails also were built in the 1930s. Major competitions came with the completion in 1938 of a Class A racing trail on a privately owned spur of Whiteface Mountain, a massive mountain standing alone at the head of Lake Placid. The run, made possible through funds donated by Lake Placid citizens, eventually had a vertical descent of 2,700 feet and a length of two miles.

In November of 1941 the voters of New York state, by a slim margin of less than 10,000 votes of two million cast, passed a constitutional amendment allowing the state to build a major ski center on Whiteface Mountain. Actual construction was postponed because of World War II. Opened in 1949 on a shoulder of Whiteface called Marble Mountain, the center consisted of a T-bar, four trails, and a log lodge. Lake Placid had now entered fully into the Alpine skiing picture, but Marble Mountain was plagued by unfavorable wind exposures and lasted only until 1958.

When Averell Harriman, who had founded Sun Valley before entering politics, became governor of New York in 1954, he used his influence to win support for an entirely new state-owned center on the main body of Whiteface. Upon voter approval of still another amendment, construction of the present Whiteface Mountain Ski Center was completed in January of 1958. The first snowmaking equipment was installed in 1961, and in 1965 a major expansion resulted in the East's longest racing trail and its greatest vertical drop—3,216 feet, more than some of the major ski areas of the West. Further improvements were made for the World University Games in 1972, and with the awarding of the 1980 Olympics a complete renovation of Whiteface's lodges and trails began, as all Alpine events of 1980 were held on this mountain.

The preparations for the 1980 Olympics brought many other changes to Lake Placid: new cross-country trails; two new ski jumps of 70 and 90 meters (the latter sporting a 262-foot-high scaffold, which, in addition to being the tallest structure between Albany and Montreal, attracted the criticism of environmentalists); a reconditioned and refrigerated bobsled run; a new speed skating oval; a fieldhouse for hockey and figure skating; and an Olympic village, built with federal funds, that would be used as a prison once the Games were over.

As in the 1932 Olympics, weather was again a problem in 1980 with only a very light snow cover when the Games began. But this time Lake Placid was ready—Whiteface was blanketed with snow made by one of the world's largest snowmaking systems; even the jumps were serviced by snowmaking equipment that could cover the hill in 24 hours.

Lake Placid's 1980 Olympics completely dwarfed the Games held there in 1932. Some 1,400 athletes competed in 38 events, with the results reported by over 3,000 members of the press. The big American victories came not in skiing but in skating and hockey—speed skater Eric Heiden's five gold medals and the stunning victory of the U.S. hockey team. In Alpine skiing, the U.S. scored only one medal—Phil Mahre's silver in the slalom—while Austria, Switzerland, Germany, Sweden and Liechtenstein dominated the events.

Beyond the results of the competitive events, the Olympics left another legacy in Lake Placid—the village is now the official Eastern Olympic Training Center, and its facilites are in constant use by Olympic hopefuls as well as by vacationists. Even before receiving this designation, Lake Placid was the home of many top U.S. skiers and coaches, especially in the Nordic events. Since 1924, about 50 Lake Placid men and women have been named to U.S. Olympic teams, 10 of them skiers. In the future, undoubtedly, there will be more.

The village of Lake Placid lies along two lakes, Mirror and Placid. Whiteface Mountain looms in the background and the 1980 Olympic fieldhouse is at the left.

Lake Placid Chamber of Commerce

The 70 and 90 meter Intervale ski jumps, built for the 1980 Olympics.

Nancie Battaglia
Lake Placid, N.Y.

CHAPTER SIX

FROM LEATHER STRAPS TO HIGH-TECH

SKI EQUIPMENT

Ski technique always has been greatly dependent on ski technology. A graphic example of this is seen in the 12-foot-long racing skis of the Sierra gold miners. Their length and shape made turning very difficult, if not impossible. Even if a Sierra racer had wished to turn, his soft boots and loose leather bindings, unlike today's boots and bindings, would have done very little to translate his body movements to his skis. A man on those skis was a passenger rather than a driver.

For thousands of years, ski technology developed at a very slow pace. Skis were made of single pieces of carved wood, sporting an upturned tip and fastened to the foot with a leather toe strap. Skiers also used single wooden poles and soft leather boots.

Classifications exist for several types of prehistoric skis, based mainly on shape. They have one thing in common, however—all were designed for cross-country transportation, not downhill running. Some of the early skis, in fact, would have been nearly worthless for skiing down a hill—several centuries ago, Scandinavian soldiers were using one long ski (for gliding) and one short ski (for kicking).

The modern downhill ski and ski binding got their start in the mid-19th century in Telemark, Norway; they contributed immeasurably to the development of downhill skiing as a sport. Unlike many other styles, the Telemark ski was long and thin and it possessed sidecut—its tip and tail were broader than its waist, which gave the ski the impetus to turn when it was set on edge. Just as important was its new binding. Instead of the old leather toe strap, Telemark's Sondre Norheim invented a binding made of twisted roots that formed a loop around the heel of the boot. This gave skiers unprecedented control over their skis and ushered in the first real downhilll turns, the telemark and christiania. These skis also were made with camber—the characteristic reverse bow running the length of the ski that distributes the skier's weight more evenly, giving stability on downhill runs.

The osier binding, invented by Sondre Norheim more than 100 years ago.
Author's collection

Some of the first ski boots were snowshoe moccasins or rubber-leather Barker boots. Here the footrest is covered with fur, its hair pointing forward to increase the "push" on the ski.
NESM

A 1900-era ski made in Holyoke, Mass. Eventually, almost all skis were modeled after those developed in Telemark Norway, in the 19th century. They featured a long graceful shape, sidecut for turning, and camber to distribute a skier's weight more evenly.
NESM

The Telemark ski was widely imitated in Europe and North America during the last part of the 19th century. Previous to that time, the early American skiers had handcrafted their own skis of their own design. Some of these skis were very specialized, such as the very long and very heavy skis of the Sierra racers, designed exclusively for straight downhill running.

The first ski factory in this country was established at St. Croix Falls, Wis., in 1888, although it is reported that during the height of the Sierra racing craze, skis could be purchased at a La Porte Cabinet shop for a pinch of gold. Another early ski company, the Strand Ski Co., established St. Paul as a center of ski manufacturing, a reputation that was enhanced with the arrival of the Northland Ski Co., which manufactured skis at St. Paul for many years. The Strand factory later moved to New Richmond, Wis.

These early skis were made from a single piece of wood—usually hickory—with wooden edges and bottoms that required wax to prevent snow from sticking. The early 1890s saw the first laminated wood skis, giving the manufacturer greater control over durability and flex, but they did not come into common use until decades later.

By 1910, according to Ted Bays in his book *Nine Thousand Years of Skis,* "cross country and jumping skis had attained the basic form that endures to this day." This form was based on the Telemark configuration, as was the downhill ski. But the downhill ski would go through many more refinements, a process that started in the 1920s when downhill running became recognized as a separate sport from Nordic skiing.

In 1928, Rudolph Lettner, an Austrian metal worker, was looking for a way to protect ski bottoms from damage and he invented the metal edge. This proved to be a very significant development. It permitted skiers to bite their skis into hard snow, giving much greater turning control and more ability to "carve"—rather than skid—through a turn.

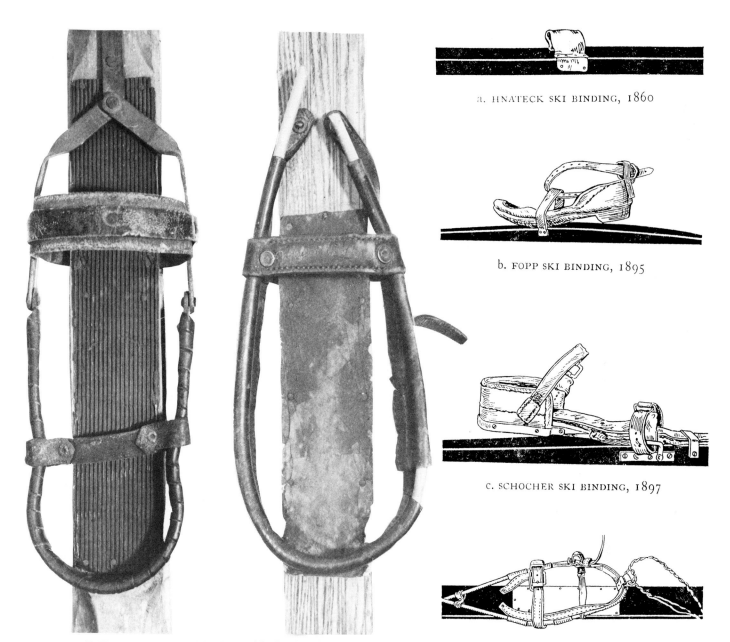

a. HNATECK SKI BINDING, 1860

b. FOPP SKI BINDING, 1895

c. SCHOCHER SKI BINDING, 1897

d. EGGENBERT SKI BINDING, 1900

A Norwegian cane binding with the bamboo encased in saddle-stitched leather. Originally, skis were held to the foot with a toe strap only. As skiers turned to downhill running and sought a better connection to their skis, the heel straps came into use, and then the cable binding.   NESM

Some very early "safety" bindings. Release bindings were first available in the late 1930s, but did not come into common use until many years later.

SALOMON BINDINGS

The Salomon "lift cable" binding, for many years the world's most popular binding. Although imported from France, Salomon bindings have been very popular among American skiers for the past 30 years. The company was founded in 1947 when Francois "Pepe" Salomon left his job as a sawmill foreman and invested his savings in a workshop which manufactured steel ski edges and was located in the heart of the French Alps at Annye. Several years later, Salomon and his family introduced their first binding in the form of the Skade releasable toe piece. Soon after, they developed the lift cable binding, which established the company as a leader among binding manufacturers. Over the years, the company has introduced a number of other innovations, including a toe piece with a double-pivot axis, the step-in competition binding, and the first toe piece that incorporated anti-shock features. Today, Salomon continues to be a leader in the binding industry.

The Saranac ski, top and bottom views. The ski was made in the Lake Placid region and is unique for the three-eighths-inch metal bar inserted in the bottom to serve as a runner. Thus it did not need a groove. Like others of the era, its binding used a leather toe strap, but the punched holes and the remains of a cord indicate that the binding may have incorporated a heel strap as well.
NESM

From there the pace quickened. Laminated wood skis became popular during the 1930s, their shape becoming increasingly refined. At the same time, bindings took on a new function. Since the beginning of ski history, bindings had been designed to hold the boot toe in place, but permit the boot heel to lift freely for cross-country, jumping, and telemark turns. As downhill technique evolved, however, and Hannes Schneider introduced the stem turn, the telemark turn (and the need for a freely lifting heel) became obsolete. Skiers using stem turns found they had more control if their heels were clamped firmly to the skis. Thus, in the 1930s, Alpine skiers adopted cable bindings that held down their heels.

Adding to the skier's control of his skis were more advanced boots. They became stiffer and heavier, although, like the high, soft boots of an earlier era, they were still made of leather and fastened with laces. Meanwhile, inventors were working on a release binding to prevent the broken legs that resulted from the stiffer boots and tighter bindings.

About the time of World War II, synthetic materials were introduced to ski technology. One of the first of these was p-tex. A plastic invented by the Swiss firm of Muller and Co. in 1946, p-tex was initially used on Holly skis and provided a running surface to prevent snow from sticking to the base.

In the last 30 years, other synthetic materials have revolutionized ski technology, which, in turn, has permitted great strides to be made in downhill technique. At the forefront of this revolution was Baltimore's Howard Head, who, about 1950, invented a successful and widely used metal ski (other metal skis had been available on a limited basis before that time). Made from aluminum, the Head skis were lighter and easier to turn than the stiff wooden skis, and their owners reported that they "snaked" over bumps. By the early 1960s, metal skis were firmly established in the American ski market.

But not for long. Ten years later, fiberglass skis were the rage. Very light and very responsive, their fiberglass construction enabled ski engineers to control closely such characteristics as damping (the ski's ability to remain in contact with the snow), overall flex, and torsional rigidity (a ski's stiffness across its breadth, which affects the way it "holds" on hard snow). Skiers also moved to shorter sizes, finding them easier to turn, although they sacrificed stability and carving ability in doing so. These shorter skis, the long-ski purists maintained, also wreaked havoc with the slopes, creating short, steep, choppy moguls.

Meanwhile, ski bindings became safer (as well as more expensive and elaborate) as release technology leaped ahead, and ski boots changed drastically. First, laces were replaced by buckles; then, in 1964, Robert Lange introduced a plastic ski boot. Nearly all manufacturers switched to plastic buckle boots, and began making them so they extended higher up the leg, a development that permitted a "sitting back" style of skiing which enabled skiers to absorb bumps.

The purpose of all these technological advances was actually quite simple. Ski boots and bindings were intended to give a skier greater control over his skis. With the new bindings, a skier was attached more firmly (and more safely) to his skis, while the stiff, high-topped boots translated the slightest leg movements directly to his edges. The skis themselves were made so they were more responsive and lively as they carved through the snow.

The result has been an enormous improvement in ski technique. In general, skiers can make quicker, tighter, better-carved turns with considerably less effort and with subtler body movements than a skier using the heavy, loose-fitting equipment and the ponderous up-and-down and rotational techniques of the past.

Below left: Fred Pieren waxing skis at Sun Valley, 1950. With the advent of sophisticated plastic bottoms, waxing for recreational skiing is no longer as important as it once was.
SV

Below right: Skis at Sun Valley, 1940s. This was before the era of step-in and safety bindings.   SV

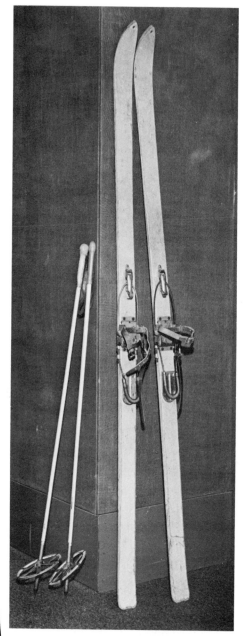

The famous G.I.-issue white skis
and poles. Thousands of these
wooden skis were dumped on the
civilian market after the war and
enabled many people to take up
the sport.   Hays Otoupalik Collection
Historical Museum
at Fort Missoula (Mont.)

Top: the Groswold Ski Co. was located for many years in Denver, Colo. Bottom: hand-shaping and edging skis at the Groswold factory.   DAM

One of the earliest ski factories in the United States was the Strand Ski Co., located in New Richmond, Wis. The upper photo was taken in 1914, the lower photo in 1925. For many years, ski factories tended to be not much more than glorified woodworking shops or converted spare rooms in some entrepreneur's house. It appears here that the Strand Ski Co. also did a brisk business in the manufacturing of canoe paddles.

Minnesota Historical Society

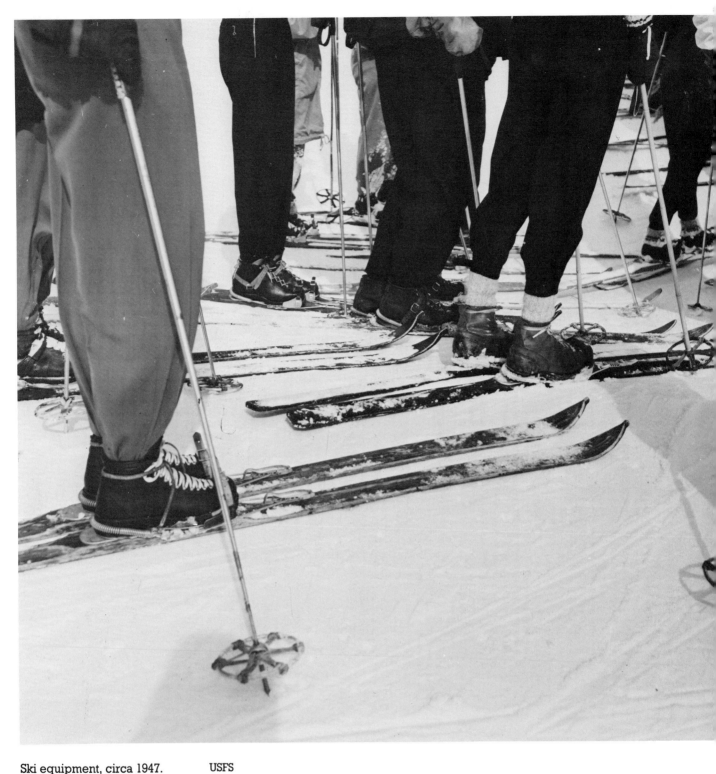

Ski equipment, circa 1947.   USFS

Two skiers prepare skis in the club room of a ski organization in Rhinelander, Wis., 1940.
USFS

An unusual ski rack on an early-1930s automobile. FH

Scenes from an early ski-equipment factory.   NSM

HEAD SKIS

In 1947, a 32-year-old aircraft engineer by the name of Howard Head spent a week skiing at Stowe. He'd only skied a few times before; though he took a liking to the sport, he found that his rental equipment felt heavy and clumsy. On the train trip from Stowe to his home in Baltimore after that week, Head started thinking about designing a new type of ski.

Head's idea was to build a metal ski—a ski, it turned out, that would revolutionize the sport. With $6,000 in savings and poker winnings, Head, a Harvard graduate who had gotten sidetracked from creative writing to aircraft engineering, purchased equipment and rented the corner of a shop in Baltimore. There, he produced his first ski, a metal sandwich of aluminum surrounding a core of honeycomb plastic.

This ski, however, had problems. It broke while instructors at Stowe were bending it with their hands, testing it for flex. The pairs that did make it to the slopes gathered heavy clumps of snow on their aluminum bottoms, and they had edges that dulled too quickly. Then those pairs broke as well.

Head went back to his shop. After many other failures, he eventually came up with a ski that employed a plywood core (which was heavier but stronger than honeycombed plastic), a bottom coated with phenolic plastic, and a spring-steel edge in addition to the sandwiched layers of aluminum.

Finally, in the spring of 1950, Head packed a pair of his latest skis up to the Headwall of Tuckerman's Ravine. There he gave them to a skier by the name of Clif Taylor, who would go on to earn his own place in the history of ski instruction. Taylor took the skis up to the top. Head, who was not a strong enough skier for the Headwall, watched as Taylor carved his way down the steep face. At the bottom Taylor announced, "They're great, Mr. Head. Just great."

At that point, says Howard Head, he knew he had the right ski.

Howard Head, inventor in the 1950s of a popular metal ski.   NSM

Howard Head examining skis at his factory near Baltimore, Md.   NESM

HART SKIS

Head was not the only American-made metal ski on the market in the 1950s. In 1955, Harry Holmberg, who had been an employee of Gregg Ski Co. in St. Paul, got together with Hartrig Holmberg and Ed Bjork to manufacture metal skis under the Hart brand name, and for a time, Hart was one of the leading names in the American ski industry.

Like Head, Hart moved its manufacturing facilities to Europe in the 1980s. Today, the major U.S.-based ski manufacturers are K-2, Olin, and Pre. K-2, based in Washington state, has been producing skis since the mid-1960s and is the largest of these.

FIBERGLASS SKIS

The first true fiberglass ski to hit the market was the Toni Sailer, introduced in the early 1960s by Fred Langendorf. The ski originally was not intended to be produced commercially—Langendorf, an engineer who happened to be working with fiberglass at the time, simply wanted to make a few pairs for his own use.

The ski was designed in 1959 and was tested that winter by Ernie McCulloch and Les Streeter. They were so excited about the fiberglass construction that they talked Langendorf into going commercial with his product.

Financed by G.M. Plastic Corp., the ski went on the market in 1966, and marked the beginning of a boom in fiberglass ski construction. At about the same time, K-2 came out with its first full fiberglass ski, the Holiday, while the French firm of Dynamic produced the first fiberglass-wrapped ski. The earlier skis had been made of molded fiberglass, but in the Dynamic construction, fiberglass was wrapped around an interior core.

SKI BOOTS

Modern ski boots are odd contraptions, with their high, plastic uppers, their buckles, and their inner linings filled with strange substances. Yet the ski boot is a strictly functional device, and its basic function is to transmit a skier's leg movements directly to his skis.

A century ago, this was not the case. Skiers wore everyday outdoor footwear, such as gum-rubber shoes, or boots made for farming, logging, or hunting. These may have been warm and comfortable, but they gave the wearer little control over his skis.

The original downhill ski boots, used in the first part of this century, resembled mountaineering boots (skiers in those days, in fact, resembled mountaineers, at least on the long climb up). The boots were made of heavy, stiff leather, and they eventually employed a stiff sole to prevent the boot from curling when it was clamped in a cable binding.

With advances in technique after World War II, boots became increasingly stiffer, but they still were made of leather, which had a tendency to break down, and lacing them properly took a lot of time and effort. In 1955, Henke introduced a buckle boot made of leather. Meanwhile, Bob Lange was experimenting with fiberglass to stiffen boots further. In 1964, Lange introduced a plastic ski boot. One of his models was adopted by European racers, who dubbed the Lange boots "les Plastiques Fantastiques." Before long, everyone was making plastic ski boots.

Later innovations included boots that used small bags of material that could be packed around the foot for a proper fit (Rosemounts), "flow" linings that conformed to an individual's foot, and foam fitting, where a skier stood in his boots while liquid foam was injected around his feet, also for a proper fit. Boots were built higher for better control over the skis, and they sported high backs that facilitated "sitting back," originally a technique used by French racers. (Skiers who wanted to sit back on the early boot models resorted to building their own high backs with materials like tongue depressors.) More recent features include adjustable forward lean and adjustable forward flex.

Early ski boots were made of leather and were relatively low and soft compared to today's models. As skiers sought more control over their skis the boots became higher and stiffer.
WASM

The Lange plastic ski boot, introduced in the early 1960s. Lange boots ushered in a new era in ski boot design as almost all manufacturers started making plastic boots. The higher, stiffer boots also changed ski technique as their owners found they had better edge control and could "sit back," like the French racers, to absorb bumps and to shoot out of tight slalom turns.
WASM

1965 LANGE SKI BOOT

Up until this plastic boot hit the slopes all boots were mostly leather. The Lange boot started a revolution in both technique and boot design.

Several generations of ski boots on display at the Denver Art Museum, 1984. They range from the soft, high, leather boots worn by the very early skiers to the stiff, high, plastic boots worn by modern skiers. The Rosemount boot on the far right was the first form-fitting boot on the market, introduced in 1965.
DAM

SKI BINDINGS

In 1938, Hjalmar Hvam, a well-known Norway-born skier and jumper, broke his leg while skiing at Mount Hood, Ore. A year later, Hvam broke the same leg. This time, however, he decided to do something about it.

Hvam took a French idea, elaborated on it, and in 1939 came out with the first release binding—the Hvam Saf-ski binding. From there, release bindings began to catch on, and other manufacturers came out with their own variations. But it wasn't until the 1960s that release bindings became almost universally popular, in part because some skiers initially believed a released ski thrashing about was more worrisome than a possible leg break.

The first generation of bindings used a release toe piece and a cable heel that incorporated forward release. Then, in 1950, the first step-in binding was introduced, the New Jersey-made Cubco. A fairly simple device, it used metal brackets attached to the boot toe and heel which snapped into spring-loaded clips mounted on the skis. At about the same time, Utah's Earl Miller brought out a step-in binding which also required plates on the boots. Both the Cubco and Miller bindings featured forward, backward, and sideways release.

Since about 1960, binding technology has evolved rapidly. The plate binding is used by many skiers, but the step-in is more popular, with companies like Marker, Tyrolia, Salomon, Look, and Geze (none of them American) the leaders in the binding field.

Although skiers can still break a leg on today's bindings, they are much safer than the release bindings of an earlier era. Both skiers and manufacturers have become much more safety conscious, and a manufacturer who is, not risks lawsuits from injured skiers who are.

Some of the innovations in the last two decades include anti-friction pads, designed to let the boot slip easily out of the binding when it releases; "ski brakes," a spring-loaded arm that jams into the snow when the ski releases from the boot, replacing the old "safety straps"; and "anti-shock" features, permitting the boot to move a bit out of the binding when the ski is jarred, and then snapping it back into place, thus preventing the binding from releasing too easily when the skier encounters rough terrain or a jarring turn.

This last feature has received a lot of attention from binding manufacturers. They look for a binding that excels at distinguishing between a quick shock to the ski imparted by the terrain and the kind of shock (as in a fall) that could break a leg. The binding of the future, according to some observers, will make this distinction with an electronic brain.

Today's American binding manufacturers include Spademan and Burt. The binding market, like the ski market, is now dominated by European companies, but it is significant that the releasable binding was first developed in America. In the last 50 years, many of the important developments in ski-equipment design took place in this country. They include Hvam's releasable binding, Howard Head's metal ski, Ed Scott's metal poles, Fred Langendorf's fiberglass ski, and Bob Lange's fiberglass boot.

The 1951 Hanson binding, the forerunner of the popular Miller binding of the 1960s and 1970s.
NSM

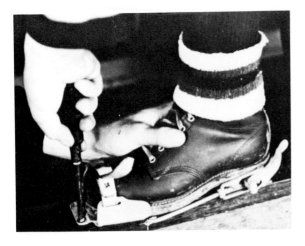

An early non-releaseable binding with a toe-iron and heel hold-down.
NSM

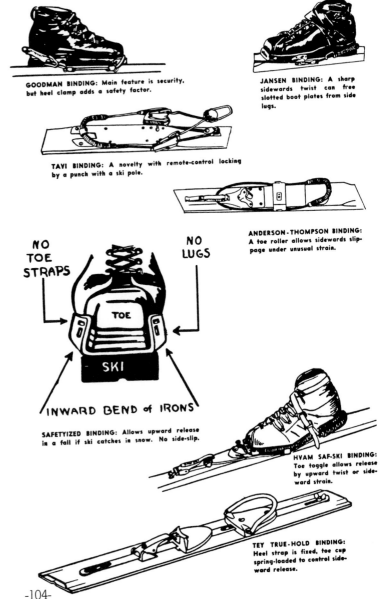

GOODMAN BINDING: Main feature is security, but heel clamp adds a safety factor.

JANSEN BINDING: A sharp sidewards twist can free slotted boot plates from side lugs.

TAVI BINDING: A novelty with remote-control locking by a punch with a ski pole.

ANDERSON-THOMPSON BINDING: A toe roller allows sidewards slippage under unusual strain.

NO TOE STRAPS

NO LUGS

TOE

SKI

INWARD BEND of IRONS

SAFETYIZED BINDING: Allows upward release in a fall if ski catches in snow. No side-slip.

HVAM SAF-SKI BINDING: Toe toggle allows release by upward twist or sideward strain.

TEY TRUE-HOLD BINDING: Heel strap is fixed, toe cup spring-loaded to control sideward release.

6° 7.30 A. M.   Fine.

Went skeeing a little
over to Bradley's. Very
fast on the steep hill.
Studied quite a little.
My idea of a skee now is
one between 8 & 9 ft. long.
at least 5½ in. wide. Today
I cut my shoes because my
feet project out over the
sides. As stiff as possible
in back and still have it
balance down. Wider at
front than back. Quite
thin and bendy at front.
Grooved of course! nearly
to the back end, am not
so sure about the front
end. I wonder what my
idea will be a year from
now!?!

A page from the diary of Fred Harris, founder of the Dartmouth Outing Club.   NESM

Hvoom with Hvam
and have no fear

In 1937 I broke my leg.

In 1938 the same leg broke.

In 1939 I invented the safe ski binding. No more broken legs. So I thought.

So in 1939 I fell through the finish gate and my leg broke after I won a down-hill race.

However, this is how lucky a dumb Norwegian gets. My leg was not healed from before. "Hjalmar," the doctor told me, "you are lucky we don't have to amputate. Only a little piece of bone was holding together."

Since then I never break a leg.

Why?

This is bragging, but it is true.

I had invented my Hvam safe ski bindings.

My Hvam bindings always release before my bones break. That is what Hvam bindings do best in the world. When I ski hard and fast they do not come off, even when my skis chatter. When I fall they release. Many great racing skiers now use Hvam bindings. I will not say their names because they are my friends and I will not take their advantage. Just look down next time.

It is safe to say: There is no better binding than a Hvam. If you must adjust the binding, possibly you adjust it too loose the first time and too tight the next time. The Hvam binding is automatic. I put in the correct tension with a precision torque screwdriver.

Some bindings look like blacksmith machinery. The Hvam binding is very small and very beautiful.

Hjalmar Hvam, inventor of the first safety ski binding, photographed near Alta, Utah by George Schwartz.

Now. Will the Hvam bindings keep improving? I don't think so, but maybe. I am working on something that I want to show you at the ski show.

My friends say, "Hjalmar, you are the luckiest man in the world. You are in the ski business and yet you get to ski all the time."

This is true. I am lucky. In 1939 I invented the Hvam safe ski binding, and my leg broke for the last time.

United States representatives: Johnny Seesaw's, Peru, Vt. (New York: Bill Parrish. Denver: Phil Clark, Jr. Los Angeles: Bill Halstead. Seattle: Bob Ramsay. San Francisco: Bob Ramsay.)
Canadian representative: Gresvig Ltd. Vera Hvam every place else.
Australian representative: Martire Enterprises, Sydney.

Hjalmar Hvam
Saf-Ski bindings

Rte.1, Box 404, Beaverton, Oregon

SKI POLES

For centuries, skiers carried a single heavy wooden pole, which was used for pushing, for balance, and, when dragged or straddled, for braking.

At one point, two poles were thought to get in the way when a skier was running downhill, but during the early 1900s, two poles came into style. For decades these were made of bamboo, which varied in length according to the technique of the day, and which were equipped with large floppy baskets.

In 1959, Sun Valley's Ed Scott changed all that with his aluminum alloy pole that was much lighter and had a much better balance than the old bamboo poles. Since then, lightweight metal poles have become the industry standard.

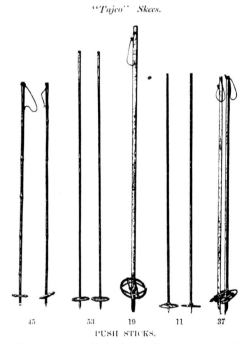

"Tajco" Skees.

45   53   19   11   37

PUSH STICKS.

No skidor is well equipped unless he has at least one pair of push sticks and one long stick to use as occasion may require.

No. 45. Bamboo. Rattan cups, steel points, set in ferruled ends. Rawhide wrist straps.   4¼ ft. long, per pair, $1.50

No. 53. Selected straight grained, light, tough wood. Hardwood cups, steel points set in ferruled ends.   5 ft. long, per pair, $1.50

No. 19. Long single stick. Useful in coasting as brake and for steering, also to assist in hill climbing. Selected straight-grained ash stock, steel shod, with rattan cup. Rawhide wrist strap.   6 feet long, each, $1.50

No. 11. Selected straight-grained, light, tough wood with rattan cups. Steel points set in ferruled ends.   5 ft. long, per pair, $1.50

No. 37. Special lock-cup push sticks, selected straight-grained ash stock, steel shod tips, rattan lock cups. Locking device enables sticks to be locked together and used as a single guide stick or taken apart and used as pair. Rawhide wrist straps.   4½ ft. long, per pair, $3.00

CHAPTER SEVEN

WHAT GOES UP...

SKI LIFTS

For decades, rope tows were the mainstay of uphill transportation. They are still used in some smaller areas. Caberfae Ski Area, Mich., circa 1950s.
Michigan State Archives

In the beginning, you walked. For decades skiers got along without lifts, the long slog up being the price one paid for a ride downhill.

There was a certain sweaty freedom to those days. It was all very simple—you just found the nearest skiable snow-covered hill, and then you started climbing. One could argue, in fact, that the ski lift gave birth to modern organized skiing. Before there were lifts, only a few hardy souls pursued the sport, and they didn't really need ski areas to do so.

.The invention of ski lifts, however, marked the beginning of skiing's mass appeal and the beginning of the full-scale winter sports resort. The growing number of skiers had to travel to designated ski areas to use the new devices, and once there they needed lodging, food, night-time entertainment and a host of other diversions and services—all the fixings of a modern resort.

Of course, the lift has its disadvantages, and there are purists who shun its use. For one thing, lifts are a mechanical contrivance transporting skiers through an essentially natural setting; for another, they are expensive and tend to foster long lines and crowded and bumpy slopes. Still, whatever their drawbacks, ski lifts have one big advantage: a skier using a lift can get about 10 times more skiing in a day than one who climbs on foot.

This Ford Model A wheel, apparently modified for running a rope tow, is on display at Donner State Park in California. According to some accounts, a group of Truckee, Calif., skiers operated a rope tow at Donner Summit as early as 1932. If so, the device would be the earliest known rope tow operation in North America.　　Bill Clark, WASM

The first documented U.S. lift—possibly the first in the world—to be constructed primarily for winter sports was the one at Hilltop, Truckee, Calif., for the 1913-14 season. It was originally intended to haul toboggans up the north-facing slope just south of town, but as skiers increasingly came to use it, subsequent lifts that were built in the area became more and more adapted to skiers. This is the same year the Truckee Ski Club was organized, and its members enthusiastically cooperated with the Southern Pacific Railroad to develop winter sports. The lumber industry was in a decline at this time and winter sports were seen as a stimulus to the local economy. The steam engine that powered this lift and the cable that hauled the customers were salvaged from one of the dismantled lumber plants.
Bill Berry

The age of the ski lift didn't really begin until the 1930s, but a few lifts existed before that time. Aerial tramways, for instance, had been used for mining and other purposes since at least the mid-1600s. Some of them may have been used by skiers—like the California boys with skis who were reportedly riding ore-bucket conveyor belts up the mountainsides back in the 19th century.

There has been some controversy about when and where the first ski lifts were built. According to some historians, a rope tow was in operation in Austria in 1905, although it was not used exclusively by skiers. The first U.S. lift apparently was built in 1913 at Truckee, Calif., on the north shore of Lake Tahoe. On a 500-foot slope behind a railroad hotel, Truckee Winter Sports built a steam-engine-powered lift that consisted of two toboggans, one attached to each side of a continuous cable loop. One sled was hauled uphill while the other went down, a concept that would find expression in a number of later lifts. Originally this lift was built to haul tobogganists, but it was soon adopted by skiers.

The Truckee lift was not the beginning of a trend. No more lifts are known to have been built in the U.S. until the 1930s, although in 1915 members of the Dartmouth Outing Club discussed an "engine to haul men up the gully on skis during the Carnival." (According to club minutes, they dismissed the idea as "impracticable." Rather, it was the Europeans, avid skiers even then, who were pioneering ski lifts in the 1920s and the early 1930s.

In addition to climbing, the Europeans frequently used their existing railroads to get up mountainsides. Then, in 1927, an aerial tram—intended for skiers—was built in Switzerland. A year later France built the first surface lift at Chamonix, though it is not clear just what type of device this was.

In 1932, Gerhard Mueller, a Swiss, filed for a patent on a rope tow powered by a motorcycle engine. This lift apparently inspired others across the Atlantic, for on Jan. 2, 1933, North America's first rope tow opened at Shawbridge, Quebec.

Built by Alec Foster, it consisted of a continuous rope powered by the rear wheel of a propped-up Dodge automobile. While the design was hardly sophisticated, this type of automobile-powered rope tow was relatively easy and inexpensive to build. Similar devices soon appeared throughout North America.

Gilbert's Hill, near Woodstock, Vt., is generally credited with the first rope tow in the U.S., although it is by no means certain that a few others did not exist before Gilbert's tow opened in 1934.

The Truckee haulback lift in 1915, after it was improved. Upper photo shows detail of a sled being hauled back on the trestle. The cable ran up the center, with vertical cogs that engaged the sleds. The sophistication of this apparatus suggests that it may have been copied from an earlier, more primitive rig, perhaps a mine lift.   Bill Berry

The first rope tow in North America was built in 1933 by Alec Foster at Shawbridge, Quebec. The device was described in the January 1933 SKI BULLETIN of Boston:

"On Sunday, January 1, 1933, it was just a shaken-down, snowed-under old derelict of a Dodge, parked in the snow off to one side at the bottom of the "big hill," at Shawbridge, with two men tinkering away in the 15 below zero atmosphere. On Monday, January 2, 1933, it was the answer to the down-hill skirunner's prayer. Not a funicular, but better, a 2,000 foot endless rope, passed through blocks at the top and bottom of its span of two thirds of the hill, and around a special hub on the rear axle of the above mentioned Dodge. No schedules, no wait for the next train, just a constantly moving tow at about 15 miles per hour, which the skiers with the "price" could grab, at whatever part of the hill the desire to climb struck his fancy. Five cents a trip or fifty cents a day. Although there were halts for cooling the motor and greasing the blocks, a skier with this aid could easily have taken more down hill running than his legs could happily absorb.

Author's collection

An engine from a Model T Ford was used to power the Gilbert's Hill rope. Rope tows like this were relatively inexpensive and easy to build. The first type of ski lift in common use, they would revolutionize the sport of Alpine skiing. Woodstock Historical Society

First Ski-Tow in United States built by Mr. White Cupboard Inn

Gilbert's Hill, near Woodstock, Vt., has been credited with the first rope tow in the United States. It opened in January 1934.

Even before the advent of the rope tow, Woodstock was a noted summer and winter sports resort for East Coast residents. One of the several inns at Woodstock, the White Cupboard, remained opened during the winters in the early 1930s. Owned and operated by Robert and Elizabeth Royce, it became a haven for skiers as well as the birthplace of the U.S. rope tow.

One day early in January 1934, three young New York businessmen on a skiing holiday suggested to Elizabeth Royce that the Royces find a way to transport skiers uphill. Mrs. Royce had heard about Foster's rope tow up in Quebec, and the Royces decided to try something similar. The New Yorkers put up $100 each for the project, while the Royces rented, at $10 for the season, a former sheep pasture owned by Clinton Gilbert. They also hired a local inventor, David Dodd, to design the lift.

A few weeks and $500 later the device was ready. Its power source previously had been housed under the hood of a Model T Ford truck, and it employed a system of pulleys that held 1,800 feet of rope, running in a continuous loop from the base to the top of Gilbert's Hill. On Jan. 28, 1934, three local boys—Robert Bourdon, Lloyd Brownell, and Buster Johnson—took the first rides up the lift.

With the addition of several more rope tows on other local hills in the next few years, Woodstock became a skiing center. The best known of the local ski areas was Suicide Six.

Operated by Bunny Bertram, who had been a student at nearby Dartmouth and who stayed with the area for 25 years, Six was a favorite among racers, as its slopes were relatively long and steep and Bertram welcomed the competitors. The hill's electric-powered rope tow was as challenging as its slopes—the 1,850-foot-long tow was very steep, hauling the skiers up 650 vertical feet at a speed of about 20 mph. As one skier reminisced, "Anyone riding this tow had the feeling of being pulled straight up into the air."

Rope tows like the one at Suicide Six were notorious for the strain they put on one's arms, but they did give the user the opportunity to do some serious skiing. For example, Harold Codding set a record at Six when, in one hour, he made 30 trips up the rope tow. The 30 runs he made down in that hour were the equivalent of skiing down a mountain nearly 20,000 feet high with a run of about 15 miles.

A modern view of Gilbert's Hill.
Woodstock Historical Society

-112-

A skier could find almost as many thrills on a rope tow as he could on the trails. Sometimes ropes twisted and could snag loose clothing, as this skier demonstrates. Scarves, for obvious reasons, were to be avoided. Whitman National Forest, Ore., 1941.   USFS

This rope tow mechanism, located at Hyde State Park, N.M., was built by the Civilian Conservation Corps. The CCC, established in 1933 as a Depression-era work program, was responsible for constructing dozens of ski areas across the country.   NA

The Mount Gunstock Ski Hoist, New Hampshire's first rope tow and second in the U.S., was the longest rope tow ever built. Rider is Hollis Phillips, winner of the first American Inferno, 1933.
                                   NESM

Fred Pabst, pioneer ski-area developer and ski-lift builder.
NSM

While Woodstock was getting underway as a winter sports center, ski lifts were being built elsewhere in the country. As early as 1933, the Auburn Ski Club was discussing the possibility of building a lift on California's Tunnel Mountain at what is now Cisco Ski Hill near Lake Tahoe; possibly the lift was built the same year. Also in California, Yosemite Park's Badger Pass Ski Area installed an "automatic" lift in the winter of 1934-35. Powered by an electric motor, it consisted of a steel cable attached to a large toboggan that could carry six people.

Back East, the Dartmouth Outing Club built the first continuous drag lift, the J-bar, in 1935 on Oak Hill in Hanover, N.H. With 50 J-shaped bars dangling from a steel cable, it hauled 400 skiers an hour up the 350-foot-high hill, each ride up taking about three minutes. The following year Fred Pabst, founder of Big Bromley ski area in Vermont, installed J-bars of his own design (some accounts say he invented the J-bar) at Wausau, Wis., and Peru, Vt., and a few years later the nation's first T-bar was put into use at Pico, Vt.

T-bar at Badger Pass, Yosemite National Park, Calif. Badger Pass was one of the West's first well-known ski areas.
Yosemite National Park

The nation's first T-bar was installed at Vermont's Pico Ski Area in 1940.
Vermont Ski Area Association

"Ski barges" enjoyed a brief vogue back in the rope-tow era. If they were not necessarily more efficient than the rope, they were certainly more relaxing. Bear Gulch area, Targhee National Forest, Idaho, March 1941. USFS

Backcountry transportation. The "Weasel," a treaded vehicle, was developed by the U.S. Army for winter warfare during World War II. Medicine Bow National Forest, Wyoming, 1945. USFS

Man's ingenuity knows no bounds. This "snow scooter," constructed in Durango, Colo., weighed 450 pounds and could travel 60 to 70 miles per hour over good snow. Machines like this are still used in some remote, snowbound ranching areas of the American West. Circa 1941. USFS

Of all these innovations in lift design in the late 1930s, one stands out above the rest. It was a device that brought skiing into the modern age.

In 1935, Averell Harriman, chairman of the board of Union Pacific Railroad, was building America's first major winter sports resort at Sun Valley, Idaho. He called upon the UP's engineers in Omaha, Neb., to come up with a design for Sun Valley's ski lifts.

The engineers tinkered with J-bars, trams, and other lifts then in use, but one engineer, James Curran, came up with a totally new design. Curran had once designed an endless cable, fitted with hooks, that unloaded bunches of bananas from South American fruitboats. Curran figured that the hooks holding bananas could be replaced with chairs holding skiers.

Curran's scheme got a cool reception from most of the UP higher-ups until Charlie Proctor, a former Dartmouth skier who had been hired as a Sun Valley consultant, came to Omaha to review plans for the lifts. Curran managed to slip the blueprint for his chair into the pile of other lift designs, and Proctor saw it. Experiments with the chair were soon underway in Omaha, and the world's first chairlifts eventually were built on Sun Valley's Dollar and Proctor mountains.

The chairlift, it turned out, was the most cost-effective way to transport skiers up many mountains. The chair caught on throughout the U.S., with many of the new lifts being built by the Riblet Tramway Co. of Spokane, Wash. Since 1896, Riblet had been building uphill transportation systems for mining operations, including a device that carried people. With a slump in mining business during the Depression, Riblet turned its attention to ski lift construction. Eventually it became the largest manufacturer of ski lifts in the nation.

These Riblet aerial tramways were used for hauling ore and were the forerunners of the modern chairlift. These trams were constructed in the early 1900s in British Columbia. Headquartered in Spokane, Wash., Riblet would eventually be the nation's largest manufacturer of chairlifts.

Riblet Tramway Co.

Riding a Riblet ore bucket. Clearly, these
buckets were not designed for skiers.

Riblet Tramway Co.

Opposite: Testing a new idea. The world's first chairlift was installed on Dollar Mountain in Sun Valley, Idaho, in December 1936. The Union Pacific Railroad, builder of the resort, had given its engineers the task of designing a system to get skiers up the mountain. James Curran, a bridge engineer, had conceived the idea for the chairlift from his observations of mono-cable conveyor systems used to load banana boats in the tropics. In place of hooks carrying bananas he substituted chairs carrying skiers. He experimented with the idea (see photo) at the UP's railroad shops in Omaha, Neb. Needing to know the speed at which a chair could scoop up a skier, he built a boom on the back of a pickup truck and suspended a chair from it. He then drove the truck alongside the skier. Curran's idea brought this business of uphill transportation into the modern age.

SV

FIRST CHAIRLIFT

John E.P. Morgan was the first to test the prototype of the chairlift rigged up at the Union Pacific's railroad shop in Omaha. At the time, Morgan was serving as assistant to the chairman of the board of the UP (Averell Harriman) and was closely involved with the building of Sun Valley. The following is his account of the chair's first test run in Omaha:

"In early July 1936 I went to Omaha to test out the 'getting on and off the chair.' Glen [Trout, the UP's chief bridge engineer] produced a pair of wooden skis, but as these will not slip on concrete, I went up town and bought a pair of roller skates so that my feet would not be stuck to the ground. We then ran the truck up and down the shops in Omaha (July temperature 100 degree plus) at various speeds to test the ease of having the chair pick us up and then getting off. Several people tried the roller skates and we chose a speed which seemed reasonable for chairs to move at. From this point on the whole project became an engineering piece of exploration with the help of American Steel and Wire, and many others, as to spacing of chairs, angles of climb, locations on Dollar and Proctor mountains. We tried to keep the chairs and line fairly close to the ground but even at that we scared many people at first. . .

"When Dollar Mountain lift was opened in December 1936, my own wife and daughter would not get on the moving chair. So, at first we had to stop the lift for each passenger to get on or off. This, of course was not the idea at all—very soon skiers caught the idea, forgot their fears and began riding the chairs as they were intended."

The world's first double chairlift was built in 1946 by the Riblet Tramway Co. on Mount Spokane, Wash., for the Spokane Ski Club.

Riblet Tramway Co.

New Hampshire was the scene of other ski lift innovations. At North Conway, George Morton, a local mechanic working in his spare time, invented a contraption called the Skimobile, which was financed and built by Harvey Gibson in 1938 at Mount Cranmore.

The Skimobile transported skiers in 150 individual cars equipped with rubber tires which ran along a steel track mounted on a long wooden trestle. In 1939, a second trestle with 60 cars was added. The Skimobile is perhaps the oldest original ski lift operation in the nation. The Skimobile design also inspired a similar lift in 1959 at The Homestead in Hot Springs, Va., but this lift has since been replaced by a chair.

Mrs. Vernon Taylor (known as "Nose Dive Annie") prepares to take the first ride on Stowe's first chairlift, 1940.

Vermont Ski Areas Association

Skimobile with New Hampshire's Presidential Range in the background, March 1940.   LC

Skiers on Mount Cranmore with the Skimobile on the left, March 1940.   LC

The Mount Cranmore Skimobile at North Conway, N.H.

NA

North America's first aerial tramway for skiers began operations in 1938 on Cannon Mountain at Franconia Notch, N.H. It carried almost seven million passengers to the 4,200-foot summit before a new tram was built in 1980.   USFS

Aerial tramways also had a vogue in the U.S. in the 1930s. Initially, trams were used for non-skiing operations, such as the tram constructed by sculptor Gutzon Borglum to haul equipment and workers to the top of Mount Rushmore. Then, in 1938, two well known skiers of the era, Roland Peabody and Alex Bright, developed the nation's first tram for skiers at Cannon Mountain in Franconia Notch, N.H. With a 2,000-foot rise, it had the greatest vertical of any single lift in the country; by the time it was replaced by a more modern tram in 1980, it had carried nearly seven million passengers.

The "Lafayette," one of the pair of tram cars on the Cannon Mountain tramway, is christened by the wife of New Hampshire Governor Francis P. Murphy, 1938.   NESM

The old and the new. The middle building is the original Cannon Mountain tram base terminal; on the left is the terminal for the tram built in 1980.

An original Cannon Mountain tramway car is now part of the entrance to the New England Ski Museum, located at Cannon's base.

Mt. Gunstock, Gilford, N.H., first chairlift in the East.
NESM

Building the first chairlift in the Far West at Sugar
Bowl, Calif., 1939.   Sugar Bowl

The chairlift was the most cost-effective way to haul skiers up many mountains, and chairlifts were soon being built all over the country. A 1946 view of the single chair at the Ogden, Utah, city ski area in the Cache National Forest.   USFS

Steel towers replaced the wooden structures of the first chairlifts. All the early chairs were single; then came the double chairlift, then the triple and quadruple models.   USFS

This photograph, possibly taken at Sugar Bowl, Calif., shows a good example of an automobile used to power a chairlift. WASM

Another invention was the gondola, first used in this country at the Sierra's Sugar Bowl ski area, an off-road resort that needed a way to transport skiers to its base area. Gondolas have since been installed at a number of major U.S. resorts.

There have been other new designs—the double, triple and quadruple chair; portable surface tows; the Poma (invented in 1947 by a man named Pomagalski); and the helicopter for skiing far in the backcountry. No doubt, too, the future will bring more new methods to convey skiers mechanically to the top of a mountain. In a sense, however, the business of uphill transportation has come full circle—more and more skiers are taking up backcountry touring. Like the pioneering skiers of a century ago, they are discovering a certain sweaty freedom in the long walk up.

One of Sugar Bowl's original gondola cars, now on display at the Western America SkiSport Museum. Sugar Bowl's gondola, installed in 1953, was the first to be built in the U.S. Sugar Bowl also has the distinction of constructing California's first chairlift, opened December 1939.   WASM

The longest gondola in the Western United States is located at Park City Ski Area near Salt Lake City, Utah. It transports skiers from a base elevation of 6,900 feet to an upper terminal at 9,400 feet.
                    Park City Ski Area

Helicopters provide the latest mode of uphill transportation. Their ability to fly into the remote backcountry opens up miles of untracked powder and gives skiers one of the sport's greatest thrills.

Park City Ski Area

The famous "upski" lift at Yosemite National Park's Badger Pass was constructed in 1935. It consisted of a pair of large sleds which counterbalanced each other as one was drawn up and the other went down. The lift was operated by an electric motor and was replaced in 1948 by a T-bar. This photo also shows hard evidence that liftlines are not new. As this lift could only carry six or eight passengers per trip, these people at the end of the line have some time on their hands.　　Yosemite National Park

A slightly different approach to the "upski" lift was this large barge at Yosemite. It was self-contained with a gasoline motor in the center that operated a drum around which the cable was wound and unwound as the barge went up and down the hill. It did not work well.

WASM

Snocats provided uphill transportation for summer skiing at Mount Hood, Ore.　　USFS

CHAPTER EIGHT

GETTING TO THE FUN

SKI TRAINS AND OTHER TRANSPORTATION

A 1939 Boston and Maine ski-train poster.   NESM

These days, it is relatively simple to get to ski areas, be it by interstate highway, jet airplane, bus, four-wheel drive, rail, or, in the case of Canada's high-mountain, deep-powder resorts, helicopter.

Transportation to a ski area was not always so easy. In the early years of this century, when downhill skiing was in its infancy, the automobile was hardly a reliable means of getting somewhere in winter. The roads, where they existed, were even worse.

Rail was the transportation of choice for skiers heading to many of America's early ski resorts; the railroads, in turn, promoted their services to skiers. As early as 1867, the Central Pacific Railroad was advertising an excursion into the California mountains to "see the Sierras clad in wintry garb"—perhaps these passengers also caught a glimpse of those wild Norwegians sliding down hills on 12-foot-long boards. By about 1915, there was a resurgence of winter sports in California's Sierra, and the Southern Pacific was offering trips up to Truckee, where the railroad hotel stayed open all winter and where local residents had established a fledgling ski and winter sports industry. Trains were the only way to get there in winter.

In the 1930s and 40s, during the early boom years of downhill skiing, "snow trains" became very popular on the East Coast, and they still are fondly remembered. They hauled skiers from large metropolitan areas such as Boston and New York to the little New England ski villages in Vermont, New Hampshire, and western Massachusetts, offering both day trips and overnight stays. These areas, certainly, were accessible by car, but the trains provided an easy and comfortable trip, as well as a very sociable time on the way up. Some trains featured accordion music and dancing in the aisles, along with such practical services as rental equipment for the first-time skier.

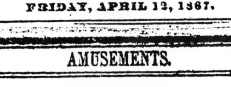

SACRAMENTO DAILY UNION.

FRIDAY, APRIL 12, 1867.

AMUSEMENTS.

GRAND EXCURSION

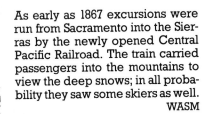

TO THE SNOWY MOUNTAINS!

THE CENTRAL PACIFIC RAILROAD COMPANY, having been earnestly solicited by many citizens to run an Excursion Train to the Mountains while the snow is still at its greatest hight, and thus afford an opportunity for ALL to see the Sierras clad in wintry garb, will,

On Sunday, April 14th,

Run an Excursion Train from Sacramento to Cisco and return, One Hundred and Eighty-six Miles,

At the Low Fare of Three Dollars!

Tickets from Auburn and all Stations west at $3; from Colfax and Stations east at $2.

This will probably be the only opportunity this season to enjoy, at so cheap a rate, the "swift transition" from the flowers of the valley to the "Arctic realm of the Sierras."

Cisco is 5,980 feet above the level of Sacramento, or 680 feet over a mile in perpendicular hight, and there is now a greater depth of snow than was ever before known, and the Scenery between Colfax and Cisco is grand beyond conception.

The Tickets will be ready for sale on and after Thursday—number limited to 2,000. Passengers not provided with Tickets will be charged $4.

Cars will leave Sacramento at 8 A. M.; Junction, 8:45; Rocklyn, 9; Pino, 9:15; Newcastle, 9:50; Auburn, 10:05; Clipper Gap, 10:20; Colfax, 10:50; Gold Run, 11:20; Dutch Flat, 11:30; Alta, 11:40; arrive at Cisco at 1:20. Returning, leave Cisco at 2:30.

a9-td   C. CROCKER, Superintendent.

As early as 1867 excursions were run from Sacramento into the Sierras by the newly opened Central Pacific Railroad. The train carried passengers into the mountains to view the deep snows; in all probability they saw some skiers as well.
WASM

Below and opposite: Skiers arriving in the early morning on the weekend "Ski-meister" train at North Conway, N.H., March 1940.
LC

Skiers unloading somewhere in the "snow country" from a Boston and Maine ski train, 1930s. NA

One of the most popular excursions was run by the Boston and Maine Railroad, leaving Boston's North Station every Saturday morning and taking skiers to New Hampshire and Vermont. The return trip was made Sunday evening, giving the skier almost two full days on the mountain.

In a late 1930s brochure listing its new winter schedules, the railroad advertised that "EVERY day is Fun Day during the winter . . ." and listed the attractions of its service: "By train you travel in warm comfort. You have no traffic worries. You get there faster, have more time to spend out of doors and no after-dark driving homeward on icy or storm-swept roads. You have fun, with safety, enroute. You can laugh at the sudden sleet storms, the unexpected blizzard, the dangerous icy roads, as you ride in warm comfort with the Boston and Maine engineer as your chauffeur."

The fares were reasonable. Boston to Lancaster, N.H., was a $5 round trip in 1938, and one-day round trips to closer areas ranged from $1.75 to $2.75.

Snow trains also ran in Colorado, taking skiers from Denver to ski areas to the west that were located along the tracks of the Rio Grande. In the Midwest of the 1930s, ski pioneer and lift-builder Fred Pabst was running a snow train from Chicago and Milwaukee to northern Wisconsin and Upper Michigan featuring a bar car, dining car, dance car, juke box and four concertina-playing Austrians dressed in lederhosen. Patrons had plenty of time to dance on this day trip—the journey to Ironwood took six and a half hours each way, broken up by a half-day's skiing.

In California, the Southern Pacific ran a snow train to Truckee during the 1930s, advising patrons to "wear your old clothes, hiking outfits and winter sports costumes," while in Idaho, the Union Pacific was building its own ski area in the form of Sun Valley—one that would rely heavily on rail transportation.

The outbreak of World War II largely put an end to the specially designated ski trains, although some ski areas are still accessible by rail. Today, at least one line, the Alaska Railroad, still runs a ski train, taking skiers from Anchorage south 90 miles to Grandview on the snowbound Kenai Peninsula. All the passengers are cross-country skiers.

The Denver and Rio Grande ski train pulls into Winter Park, Colo.

CSM

The Boston and Maine snow train boasted a "service" car in 1929. Many of the other excursions also provided equipment for the novice skier.   NESM

Interior of the Boston and Maine "service car." NESM

The New York Central ran snow trains to some areas in Michigan before World War II. This train is unloading skiers at Grayling in northern Michigan, January 1940.   Michigan State Archives

Socializing on a ski train, 1936.
Author's collection

Snow-train crowd ready for a day
on the slopes.   NESM

The Alaska Railroad ran excursions
to Grandview on the Kenai Peninsula for the benefit of servicemen
stationed in Alaska during World
War II. This view is from 1944.
Grandview is still the destination
for a ski train which runs each year
from Anchorage.
Anchorage Historical and Fine
Arts Museum

The "Snowball Special," operated by the Southern Pacific Railroad, ran from San Francisco to Truckee starting in 1932. The run ended in 1940, when Highway 40 opened up in the winter. WASM

West Portal, near Winter Park Ski Area, Colo. CHS

A modern ski train. Some of the several hundred cross-country skiers wax their skis and shoulder their day packs after stepping off Alaska's annual ski train. The Nordic Ski Club of Anchorage charters a train to Grandview, on the Kenai Peninsula about 90 miles south of Anchorage, allowing winter-weary Alaskans a day in deep-snow country. Ken C. Brovald Anchorage, Alaska

In the 1930s, during the heyday of ski trains, domestic airline service was just coming into existence, but today airlines have capitalized on the skier traffic, and many ski areas are serviced by nearby airports. Similarly, many areas are located along interstate highways, such as I-90 east of Seattle and I-70 west of Denver, the latter at times carrying a steady stream of cars packed with skiers. One only need drive that road on a snowy, traffic-clogged Sunday night to appreciate the luxurious security of a Boston and Maine "chauffeur."

An all-too-frequent occurrence for skiers traveling over icy and snowy roads. This wreck took place somewhere in Alaska.
Alaska Historical Library

Buses, too, became popular with skiers. A 1942 ski excursion to the slopes at Independence, near Juneau, Alaska.
Anchorage Historical and Fine Arts Museum

As roads became better maintained during winter, more people traveled by car. Skiers in Maine, 1937.
Maine State Archives

Skiers poured into Woodstock, Vt., by car and by rail (to White River Junction) in the late 1930s and early 40s. In 1940, when this photo was taken, the area had nine ski tows.
LC

A ski outing in 1923 at St. Mary's Lake, Colo. Ski racks apparently were not in general use at the time.
DPL

CHAPTER NINE

DRESSING THE PART

A HISTORY OF SKI CLOTHING

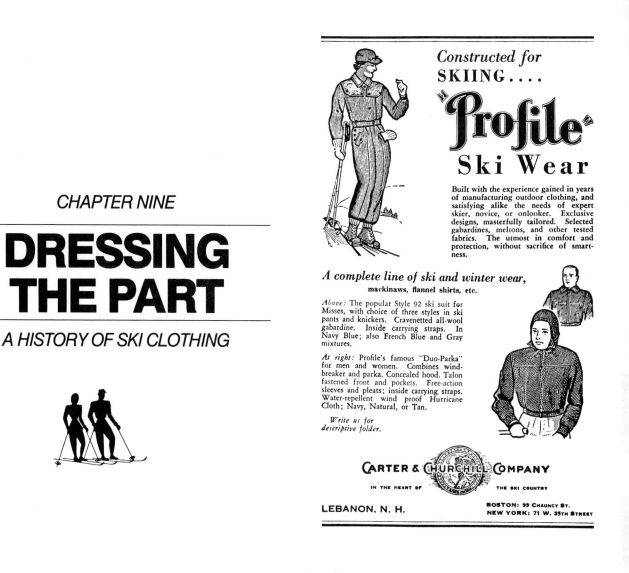

Ski and outdoor clothing is a big business today, big enough to have made an impact on the fashion world in general. Yet clothing designed specifically for skiing has only existed for about 50 years. It wasn't until the 1950s, in fact, that ski fashion acquired its trademark "sleek" look, a change that has added considerably to the aesthetics of the sport. Previously, skiers were big on baggy woolens.

The Sierra skiers of a century ago no doubt wore whatever happened to be handy. Judging from old photographs, they favored standard workshirts and high boots covered with gaiters. In some old photos, it appears that a few skiers are wearing Levi's (the original model), a fashion trend that would undergo something of a renaissance among skiers of the 1960s.

Between the gold rush days and about 1930, skiers wore strictly functional outdoor clothing, although very little of it was designed specifically for skiing. Though they could restrict movement, woolen hunting clothes were popular, as were knickers, and, in some cases, riding breeches. Knickers provided more freedom of movement, but the neckties sometimes worn along with them certainly did not.

Women had a tough time of it at the beginning. Long, heavy skirts apparently were mandatory skiwear as late as the beginning of this century. The skirts may have preserved one's modesty (except during a fall), but they were not very functional—in the mid-19th century Sierras, newspaper accounts tell of women losing "snowshoe" races because they were "carrying too much sail." Later, in the 20th century, women started wearing knickers.

The early 1930s saw the first American clothing designed specifically for skiing. At first, these styles tended to be baggy (for movement) and woolen (for warmth). Some of the "ski pants" looked like voluminous, elongated

The latest in women's ski fashions at Breckenridge, Colo., circa 1889. This bulky clothing, obviously not designed for skiing, precluded anything but straight downhill running.   DPL

knickers, drooping down past the knee, and below them skiers wore gaiters that looked like spats. Ski parkas appeared about this time, some little more than weatherproof shells, while some heavier models featured bear-fur trimming. A lightweight double-breasted parka with a deep "V" neck also enjoyed a vogue, a style brought to this country by ski instructors from Europe, where ski fashions were somewhat more advanced.

Around World War II, the forerunners to modern ski pants appeared, sporting a tapered, non-baggy cut and a hard finish to prevent snow from sticking. This trim look was pioneered by the Sun Valley Ski Clothing Co., founded in 1938 by Lew Russfield, who grew up in New England where he took up skiing, and who had apprenticed in his father's uniform-making business.

SLALOM SKIWEAR

Slalom is America's oldest ski-wear company. Currently manufacturing clothing in a converted hospital in Newport, Vt., the company's history dates back to the 1880s, when Newport was a major link in the Northeast's railroad network. Seeing an opportunity, Benjamin Franklin Moore in 1891 founded the B.F. Moore Co. to make overalls for railroad workers.

In the late 1920s, the company, seeking diversification, decided to manufacture ski clothing, quite a gamble considering that skiing was then just getting started in the Northeast. Manufacturing under the name "Slalom," the company stayed alive over the next several decades, but did not grow large.

In 1968, when it had 20 employees, it was purchased by Profile Ski Wear. Three years later, it was sold to three partners, one of whom is the great-grandson of the founder's brother. The name was changed to Slalom Skiwear Inc., a line of water-sports clothing was added, and the company has grown considerably.

Slalom skiwear from past years.
Slalom Skiwear Inc.

This B.F. Moore Co. (Slalom) parka was described in a 1932 issue of the NATIONAL CLOTHIER:

"A fur trimmed parka made of standard weight cravenetted Irish poplin. The fur, which is genuine bear, comes in brown or black.

"The garment is designed for wear over a wool ski suit or other wool clothing. It is weather repellent, and has an inner shirt tail which tucks into the trousers, and storm tight wristlets. It comes in pongee and royal blue for men and Reseda green, pumpkin, and red for women. Men's suits are priced from $10.50 to $11.50 and the women's at $9." Slalom Skiwear Inc.

Children's ski styles, 1930s.

DAM

A variety of ski styles are evident in this post-war photo from Alta, Utah. Some of the skiers wear pants with a trimmer look, a forerunner to the tight-fitting Bogners of the early 1950s. Instructor Friedl Pfeifer is on the left.   FH

The trim look may not have been baggy, but it wasn't exactly a snug fit, either, as the pants had to be cut large enough to provide plenty of freedom of movement. All this changed, however, in the early 1950s. Using a newly invented stretch fabric, the Bogner family of Germany started producing tightly fitting "stretch" ski pants. The Bogner pants, available in a wide spectrum of colors, became the rage.

From there, ski clothing became tighter and tighter, the look getting ever sleeker until some skiers were wearing one-piece, top-to-bottom stretch outfits. Then, as stretch pants became nearly universal among skiers, there appeared a number of decidedly non-stretch fashions and fads. Blue jeans and wool shirts, for instance, cropped up among younger skiers during the rebellious late 1960s. At about the same time, many skiers started wearing big, puffy, down-filled parkas and vests, which were considerably warmer than earlier parkas.

The trend now is toward the functional yet fashionable and toward "high-tech" materials, such as fabrics that claim to be both breathable and waterproof, along with insulating layers of synthetic pile, which is supposed to keep one warm even when it's wet. One-piece ski suits—some slightly baggy, some tight, some quilted—are quite popular, and stretch pants have never lost their appeal.

Nor is it likely they will. For one thing, they allow freedom of movement; for another, they provide essential streamlining for high-speed racers. And finally, something that makes a skier look good is not willingly cast aside.

By the 1920s, women were wearing knickers rather than long skirts, a change that gave them more freedom of movement and a touch of style. Note the high boots. These women are on the outrun of the jumping hill at Genessee Mountain, near Denver, Colo. DPL

Skiers with a variety of fancy ski sweaters, Donner Summit, 1939.   FH

In 1937, at Mount Baker, Wash., there were those who preferred an older style of dress.
USFS

Cross-country skiers in Vermont with 1940s ski clothes. USFS

Erling Strom (center), one of America's first ski instructors, with an early-day ski class at Lake Placid. The dress back then had a formal touch, and skiers sometimes wore neckties. NESM

WHITE STAG

What started out as a tent and awning company in 1884 has evolved into one of the largest (and, along with Slalom, one of the oldest) manufacturers of ski clothes in the nation.

In its early years, the Willamette Tent and Awning Co., located in Portland, Ore., manufactured sails for deepwater sailing ships, as well as hatch covers, tarpaulins, deck awnings, cordage, tents, and sea bags. The company's name was eventually changed to Hirsch-Weis Canvas Products (the names of its partners), and it added to its product line items for loggers, mill hands, and stockmen.

Its first clothing item was a rugged, stiff rainsuit made from sailcloth that had been dipped in paraffin, a suit that acquired the name "tin pants" and "tin coat" due to its exceptional rigidity. As the company grew, it diversified into mackinaws, gloves, saddlebags, and other items.

In 1929, Harold S. Hirsch, son of the founder and an enthusiastic Dartmouth skier, started a new outdoor apparel branch, adopting the name White Stag ("weis" meaning "white" in German, "Hirsch" meaning "male deer"). Young Hirsch's plan was to make clothing for skiers.

At the time, of course, ski clothing essentially was unheard of in this country, and skiing itself was hardly known to most Americans. But Hirsch figured skiers needed something more functional and fashionable than the standard outdoor clothing then in use.

He made his first clothing—jumping suits—for ski clubs, then started selling to ski shops and department stores around the nation. The business grew and by World War II, White Stag was offering ski pants in wool gabardine, whipcord, and whiptex, as well as poplin jackets, wool sweaters, and other items. During the 1940s, in order to operate 12 months a year, the company expanded into clothing for all seasons, and today it offers an extensive line of men's and women's sportswear.

The original factory of the Hirsch-Weis Manufacturing Co., located in Portland, Ore. This was the forerunner of the present White Stag Co. Oregon Historical Library

WHITE-STAG SKI TOGS

All skiwear courtesy of White Stag.

Button-front ski suit with front slash pockets. Made in 1941 for skiing but it was quickly adopted by "Rosy-the-Riveter" during World War II for shipyard and air-craft plant work.

Wool knickers with watch pocket in waistband. Button-close fly. Baggy knees for freedom, buckle strap fits snugly below the knees.

Reversible parka.

Ski jacket made for the Skyliners Ski Club, Bend, Ore., in 1932. "Bobbed" length and laced side openings. Slip-over style with laced front. Made of wool. Cost was $5.75.

Tyrolean wool suit, 1930s.

Gabardine waist-coat, 1935.

Two-piece gabardine ski suit, 1942.

Swiss wool ski pants, "Plus 4" bagged ankles with knit anklets. Cost was $2.65.

Fur-trimmed jacket, hooded pop-lin, has elastic waist and zip-front pockets.

One-piece gabardine jump suit.

Portland's
WINTER SPORTS
HEADQUARTERS

. . . is now ready with one of the finest, most complete Winter Sports Departments in the West

SKIS
A complete selection from the finest imported skis to the most inexpensive skis for beginners . . . featuring the Mountain King — beautifully fashioned, hand made skis . . . that have "everything".

BINDINGS
Genuine Haug bindings now at a lower price than ever . . . and more inexpensive bindings if you desire.

BOOTS
Ski boots designed right and made right! Ranging in price from $6.95 to $14.95.

WAX
The secret of enjoying skiing is the right wax! We have your favorite Bratiie and Ostby waxes of all grades.

CLOTHING
Lighter, warmer clothing . . . in snappy new models for men and women in our Sporting Goods Department and Caliente Shop. Lower prices, too!

SERVICE
Picking the right ski equipment is so important. we've secured one of the country's best skiers to manage our department.

Lipman,
Wolfe & Co.

1932

-150-

Ski clothes on exhibit at the Denver Art Museum, 1984.   DAM

Various articles of old ski clothing.   DAM

Skiwear worn by various Olympic competitors over the last 32 years. Note the modern, skintight racing suit at center.   DAM

CHAPTER TEN

BETTER THAN A SAINT BERNARD

THE NATIONAL SKI PATROL

The National Ski Patrol was formed in the aftermath of two skiing accidents in 1936, one of them tragic.

Injuries, of course, were nothing new to the sport. Broken legs and other injuries have been a part of skiing ever since man first strapped long, leg-wrenching boards to his feet. Back in the 19th-century Sierra, for example, when Snowshoe Thompson and others were pioneering downhill skiing, the tibia became known to local doctors as "the snowshoers' bone."

But in the early days of downhill skiing, injuries were simply an accepted hazard of a sport that was the province of "daredevils." When those gold miners plunged downmountain at 80 miles per hour on 12-foot-long boards, safety was hardly foremost in their minds. Winning was.

This began to change, however, as skiing gained popularity in the 1930s. It was taken up by a much broader spectrum of the public—many of them city dwellers—whose taste for thrills was a little less extreme and whose instinct for self-preservation was perhaps a bit stronger.

Early ski patrol patches. Left: original drawing of national patrolman badge by Livingston Longfellow, July 16, 1938. Middle: second drawing by Longfellow, July 27, 1938. Right: local patrol badge, 1943.   NESM

Above: Charles Minot "Minnie" Dole. Below: Dole in his later years. National Ski Patrol

MINNIE DOLE

The father of the National Ski Patrol and the guiding light of World War II's 10th Mountain Division, Dole was born in Tyngsboro, Mass., on April 18, 1899, the son of Susan Gage Dole and Charles Thurston Dole, a paper company executive. "Minnie," so nicknamed during a stint in the service, received his early education at Phillips Academy in Andover, Mass., and earned a B.A. from Yale University in 1923.

Growing up in Andover, Dole first put on a pair of skis as a member of a Boy Scout troop, although it wasn't until years later that he started skiing seriously. When he was young he developed a love for the outdoors, partly through the influence of his mother, who was an avid mountain climber. Dole spent many summers tramping through the mountains of New Hampshire.

In 1917, Dole entered the Reserve Officer Training Corps at Andover, and a year later he joined the U.S. Army. World War I ended before he finished his training, however, and he returned to complete his schooling. At Yale he was a member of the Whiffenpoofs, then one of the best-known singing groups in the nation.

After college, Dole spent several years in the wool business, then lived for three adventure-filled years in Paris as business associate and traveling companion of a wealthy college friend. In 1929, he decided that "life had its serious aspects," as he wrote in his 1965 autobiography, and he entered the insurance business in New York City, a business he stayed in for many years. Two years later he married Jane Trowbridge Ely and they had two children, Charles Minot Jr. and Susan Trowbridge.

Dole's interest in skiing was rekindled in 1933 on a trip to Lake Placid, N.Y., and from then on he was an avid skier, seeing the sport as a means to fulfill man's longing for adventure. His skiing accident in 1936 in Stowe, Vt., and the death of a friend in a skiing accident convinced him of the need for an organized group of skiers that would promote safety and assist ski accident victims. He became director of the fledgling National Ski Patrol in 1938, a position he retained until 1950, when he was named honorary lifetime chairman of the board of trustees.

In 1939, after noting the success of Finnish ski troops battling against invading Russians, Dole came to believe that the United States also needed ski troops. In 1940 and 1941, he pushed against military inertia for the establishment of ski troops, and his efforts finally convinced Gen. George C. Marshall, Army chief of staff, to create the 87th Infantry Mountain Regiment (later expanded into the 10th Mountain Division). Dole headed the recruitment of troops, acted as an advisor, and made inspection tours of encampments, all without pay.

After the war, he remained active in the ski world, and eventually established an executive recruitment firm, from which he retired as partner in 1964. Over his lifetime, he won numerous awards, including a War Department citation in 1946, an award in 1958 for all-time outstanding patrolman, and induction into the Skiing Hall of Fame. Minnie Dole died on March 14, 1976.

Dole's original jacket is on display at the New England Ski Museum. NESM

One of those who became an active skier in the 1930s was Charles Minot "Minnie" Dole, a New York insurance broker who had spent much of his youth in the mountains of New Hampshire. In 1936, Dole, with his friend Frank Edson and their wives, traveled to Stowe, Vt., to ski Mount Mansfield. Stem-christying down the Toll Road in a rainstorm, Dole broke his ankle, and, lying in the wet snow, began to go into shock.

In the absence of an alternative, Dole's skiing partners dragged him down the mountain on a piece of tin roofing. When he was told by a doctor that he might never walk normally again, he responded, "Don't worry. I'll ski again. Just wait and see."

The broken ankle might have been toted up as just another ski injury if tragedy hadn't struck two months later. Dole was still on crutches when his friend Frank Edson entered a race on the Ghost Trail at Pittsfield, Mass. Edson lost control on a curve and hit a tree, breaking his arm in two places and fracturing four ribs which pierced his lungs. He died the following day.

Edson's death eventually led to the creation of the National Ski Patrol under the guidance of Minnie Dole. In the aftermath of the tragedy, Dole was asked by Roland Palmedo, a developer of Eastern ski areas, to head a committee that would examine ski safety. The committee's report noted, among other

A 1941 Ski Patrol safety poster.
Author's collection

Auburn Ski Club's first ski patrol,
late 1930s.   WASM

Training session at Yosemite National Park, Calif., 1942.
FH

Patrollers at Alta, Utah, in 1946.
USFS

things, that injuries were caused by skiers going too fast, especially when they were hampered by poor snow and poor visibility. It suggested that ski instruction be made more widely available, that ski clubs promote physical conditioning, and recommended that skiers be taught the ethic that habitual skiing out of control is a "disgraceful" practice.

It wasn't until two years after Frank Edson's death that a nationwide ski patrol really got its start. Small, local ski patrols existed before that time, including some that were modeled after European mountain rescue groups. (Unlike the Europeans, however, the American patrols did not charge for their services, a difference that persists to this day.)

In March 1938, Minnie Dole organized a group of patrollers from various ski mountains of the East to help with the National Downhill race on the Nose Dive trail at Stowe. The patrollers, who set up safety stations along the course using portable telephones, toboggans and other equipment, made an impression on Roger Langley, head of the National Ski Association (forerunner to the United States Ski Association). Langley and Dole were standing along the course in a bitter snowstorm, nipping from a bottle of whiskey, when Langley asked Dole if he could set up a nationwide ski patrol. Dole replied, "I'll sure as hell try."

Alta, Utah.
Utah State Historical Society

Thus was born the National Ski Patrol. Working out of the den of his Greenwich, Conn., home, Dole started the organization with a $50 contribution from the Amateur Ski Club along with a $100 loan. Dole would serve as national director of the NSPS from its inception until 1950, when he was named honorary lifetime chairman of the board of trustees.

The purpose of the patrol was both to promote safety among skiers and to provide assistance for accident victims. Thus a system of first aid was one of the first priorities. The fledgling organization called on Dr. Laurence M. Thompson of the American Red Cross who in 1938 produced a winter first-aid manual. The ski patrol and the Red Cross have worked closely ever since.

To help get the patrol off the ground, Dole also persuaded some of the nation's best-known skiers to join its ranks. These included racers from the 1936 Olympic team—Dick Durrance, Alex Bright, Al Lindley, Betty Woolsey, and Bob Livermore, who assumed major responsibility in getting the organization started. Some needed a little inducement—racer Alex Bright, who was otherwise a fine patroller, was allowed to turn his patrol parka inside out twice a day so he could indulge his taste for downmountain speed.

By 1941, the National Ski Patrol listed 1,500 volunteers working in 89 patrols which served seven geographic divisions. The members underwent training and tests, and they were divided into local patrollers, who served a specific ski area, and national patrollers, who were more highly trained and who

A toboggan used by the Black Mountain Ski Patrol, Jackson, N.H., early 1950s.   National Ski Patrol

The need for specialized equipment was obvious from the outset. Until it was developed, patrollers had to make do with what they had.
National Ski Patrol

Early use of radio communications in patrolling. A U.S. Forest Service ranger reports via ultra-high frequency radiophone, Mount Hood National Forest, Ore., 1941.
USFS

More patrol work in 1941 on Mount Hood.　　　USFS

travelled from mountain to mountain. The year 1941 also saw the first women join the patrol's ranks.

Since its beginning, the National Ski Patrol was a volunteer organization. Its members were not paid, and its services were offered without charge. As the organization grew, however, money began to be a problem, and the patrol devised a number of fundraisers. One of its few successful efforts of this era was the "Broken Bone Club," limited to skiers who had broken a bone and who, for $1.50, received a sterling silver pin. Eventually the NSPS was incorporated as a non-profit organization, and donations to it were subsequently tax-free. Currently it receives private donations from companies and individuals, but its primary income is from dues paid by its own members.

Over the years, the patrol improvised its own equipment, advancing far beyond the tin roofing that once carried Minnie Dole to safety. The devices came with names like the Crystal Mountain sled, the Cascade toboggan, and the Stevens Pass splint. Developing the equipment was hardly a formal process. For instance, the Stevens Pass splint, also known as the Staeck-Jones splint, is traditionally painted blue—that's the color Jim Staeck had on hand after painting the floor of his houseboat.

The war years were a very busy time for the National Ski Patrol. Minnie Dole and other patrollers first started thinking about using skiers in the nation's defense in 1939, inspired by the performance of Finnish skier-soldiers when the Russians invaded Finland. As described in the following chapter, the National Ski Patrol was instrumental in developing the U.S. Army's winter-warfare troops and in mountain rescue work.

The era immediately after the war brought many other changes to the NSPS. Prewar skiing had been largely a casual, weekend sport, and its practitioneers were relatively few. But with the postwar boom in skiing, which was aided in part by the thousands of returning ski troops and a flood of inexpensive military ski equipment, skiing became a big business. Resorts now operated seven days a week, and they needed patrollers who could meet that schedule. The resorts were willing to hire professional patrollers, and the volunteer NSPS accepted the professionals into the organizational ranks.

The postwar years also saw the development of the NSPS avalanche training program, organized patrolling of ski races—which was inaugurated at the nation's first FIS race in Aspen in 1950 and carried on at the 1960 Olympic Games at Squaw Valley—and the advent of a junior ski patrol program.

In the late 1950s, the NSPS, which had been a branch of the United States Ski Association (formerly the NSA), stood on its own, thus becoming an affiliate of the USSA. Currently it has a full-time executive director, a staff headquartered in Denver, and maintains a membership of over 25,000 volunteer and professional men and women patrollers.

As Minnie Dole said back in the patrol's early days: "The National Ski Patrol System is essentially a great cooperative movement organized by skiers, run by skiers, for the benefit of all skiers."

Harry Pollard, Jr., a national director of the NSPS, has long been active in ski patrol, ski club, ski area and ski organization work in the East.
NSM

Headquarters of the National Ski Patrol System in Denver, Colo.

Roll call on the morning of April 1, 1939, in front of the Timberline Lodge, Mount Hood, Ore. Note that there was no standard parka at this time. The now familiar rust-colored jacket was not widely used until 1941. USFS

Junior patrollers from the Sturgeon Bay Ski Patrol receive instruction.
Door County Advocate, Sturgeon Bay, Wis.

A 1961 photo of a patroller and a snow ranger giving first aid. Note the crossed skis planted in the snow, which have become a standard distress signal. Winter Park Ski Area, Colo. USFS

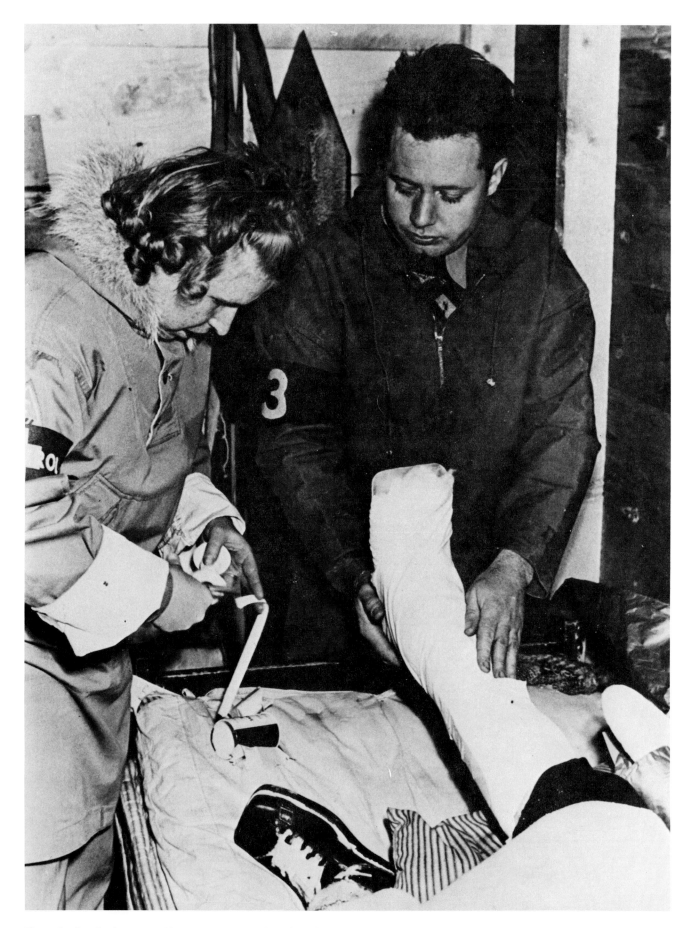

Since the beginning, patrollers have received the best in first-aid training. As early as the second year of its operation, the ski patrol was praised by the chairman of the American College of Physicians and Surgeons, who saw the patrol demonstrate traction splinting.

National Ski Patrol

CHAPTER ELEVEN

PHANTOMS OF THE SNOW

THE WAR YEARS AND THE 10TH MOUNTAIN DIVISION

A pre-war ski trooper.   USA

Men of steel and sons of Mars,
Under freedom's stripes and stars.
We are ski men,
We are free men,
And Mountains are our home.
White-clad G.I. Joe,
We're the Phantoms of the Snow.
        —from a 10th Mountain Division song

One Sunday morning in 1941, Charlie McLane, a former Dartmouth ski team captain, showed up at the gates of Fort Lewis, Wash., carrying a suitcase and a pair of skis. The sentries thought he was joking when he asked for the mountain troops. A major then read McLane's orders, and made a few phone calls.

He reported back to McLane: "Lad, you *are* the mountain infantry. You're a one-man regiment."

From a single member, in the form of Charlie McLane, the U.S. mountain troops eventually grew to a force 10,000 strong. It was a force that distinguished itself throughout its existence: during training, where a visiting Norwegian colonel called the mountain troops "the finest physical specimens in any army of the world today"; during combat in Italy, where Gen. Mark Clark said its actions were "one of the most vital and brilliant in the campaign"; and in the post-war ski industry, where many of its members left an indelible mark.

Yet McLane's reception that Sunday morning at Fort Lewis was typical of the early days of the mountain troops. The U.S. Army initially showed indifference toward the suggestion that it create a force of ski and mountain troops, and it was only after a long, hard push from civilians that the 10th Mountain Division came into being.

In the early 1930s, several years before Minnie Dole convinced the U.S. Army to establish the ski troops, the Auburn Ski Club of California was holding military ski meets. Rifles initially were used in these meets but the participants later switched to bows and arrows due to the hazard of stray bullets. WASM

Minnie Dole, the prime mover behind the creation of the U.S. Army's ski troops. NESM

Administering much of the push in those early days was Minnie Dole, founder of the then-new National Ski Patrol. Dole got the idea for ski troops one evening in February 1939 when he and three other well-known skiers of the era—Alex Bright, Bob Livermore, and Roger Langley—were sitting around a fireplace after a day's skiing at Big Bromley, Vt. As Dole describes in his autobiography, the discussion turned to the Russo-Finnish War. The Russians had invaded Finland, and Finn soldiers on cross-country skis had done a remarkable job harassing the invaders by making lightning-quick raids using Molotov cocktails and rifle fire, and then escaping on skis and ice skates.

War clouds were gathering all over the world at the time, and there was fear of an invasion of the United States. Dole became convinced that if an invasion did take place, it possibly would come from the north. He believed that if the U.S. had ski troops—like those used in Finland and other European countries—the nation would stand a better chance of repelling the attackers. At the time, however, the U.S. was training its troops largely in the southern U.S. during the winter, and had given little thought to maintaining a winter-warfare force.

Dole's initial approaches to the Army didn't meet with much success. For instance, as Dole recounts in his memoirs, he traveled to Washington at one point to meet with a colonel and try to convince him of the need for ski troops. The colonel listened for a few minutes, then pushed a button on his desk, whereupon a major entered the office. The major escorted Dole to another office, listened to the pitch, then pushed a button on *his* desk, whereupon a captain entered. The captain was told to escort Dole to the door.

Eventually, through a Yale classmate, Dole met with an aide of Secretary of War Stimson who helped arrange a meeting with Gen. George C. Marshall, Army chief of staff. Marshall gave some support to the idea, and an experimental program to test winter equipment and teach skiing was soon underway, with the National Ski Patrol System (NSPS) providing advice and help.

At first, Dole and others had envisioned a network of local ski-equipped defense patrols that would help fight an enemy invasion, but soon the concept grew to include full-fledged ski and mountain troops. Meanwhile, the idea of soldiers on skis gained more support. Wrote Colonel Muir of the 26th Infantry: "I believe ski training is an asset. Like the Texan's six-shooter, you may not need it, but if you ever do, you will need it in a hurry, awful bad."

Finally, the Army created the 87th Infantry Mountain Regiment. The National Ski Patrol was given the job of recruiting men to fill the regiment's ranks, the first time a civilian agency had been given full recruiting powers.

Many of the recruits were well-known skiers and mountaineers, some of them internationally prominent and some of them foreign-born. They included Torger Tokle, Norwegian-born champion ski jumper; Herbert Schneider, son of Arlberg system founder Hannes Schneider; Luggi Foeger, head of the Yosemite ski school; Toni Matt, champion downhiller and challenger of Tuckerman's Headwall; Peter Gabriel, originally from Switzerland and one of the finest mountaineers of the era; Walter Prager, former European racing champion and Dartmouth coach; and Austrian-born Friedl Pfeifer, another European champion and ski school director (Sun Valley, Alta, later Aspen), who had been interned after the outbreak of war and had to convince the Army he was anti-Nazi.

The ski troops also included many top former collegiate racers: Dave Harris, a top cross-country skier from Yale; Everett Bailey, University of Vermont coach; Paul and Ralph Townsend, intercollegiate combined and cross-country champions from the University of Vermont; and three former Dartmouth ski team captains—Charlie McLane, Jake Nunnemacher, and Bob Meservey. Other recruits included Paul Petzoldt of Wyoming, another outstanding mountain climber; Norm Richardson, who had set a record on the "Nose Dive" downhill at Stowe; and technical advisers like arctic explorer Vilhjalmur Steffansson.

It was an impressive group, and its credentials were not confined to athletics—the division as a whole boasted the highest proportion of college students and college graduates of any Army division, and in the 86th Regiment

87th Infantry: Constituted Nov. 15, 1941, as the 87th Infantry Mountain Regiment; concurrently 1st Battalion activated at Fort Lewis, Wash. Redesignated May 12, 1942, as the 87th Mountain Infantry. Regiment (less 1st Battalion) activated May 25, 1942, at Fort Lewis, Wash. Reorganized and redesignated as the 87th Infantry and assigned to the 10th Light Division on Feb. 22, 1944. Reorganized and redesignated as the 87th Mountain Infantry and assigned to the 10th Mountain Division on Nov. 6. 1944. Inactivated June 21, 1945, at Camp Carson, Colo.

Walter Prager, former Dartmouth ski coach and one of the earliest volunteers for the 87th Infantry Mountain Regiment, which was later expanded to the 10th Mountain Division.   NSM

Both before and during the war, a nationwide recruiting effort was mounted to find volunteers for the mountain troops. The poster pictured here was adopted from the March 1943 cover of the SATURDAY EVENING POST.   FH

85th Infantry: Constituted July 10, 1943, as the 85th Infantry. Assigned to the 10th Light Division and activated at Camp Hale, Colo., July 15, 1943. Redesignated the 85th Mountain Infantry and assigned to the 10th Mountain Division on Nov. 6, 1944. Inactivated on Nov. 30, 1945, at Camp Carson, Colo.

alone two-thirds of the men qualified as potential officer material on Army intelligence tests. Nor were all of them skiers—at one point, the Army, apparently concerned about getting too many "ski club" types, authorized the NSPS to recruit "mountaineers, loggers, timber cruisers, prospectors, and rugged outdoor men." Dole tells of receiving one application that included a single letter of recommendation (the NSPS requested three). It read: "I can highly recommend Roy Johnson. He is a Texas boy who can survive in the open, winter or summer. He needs no gun; he needs no sleeping bag. He can trap wild game without help. He's a dead shot. This I can certify, for I taught him myself. [Signed] His brother, Floyd Johnson."

Fort Lewis was the first home of the 87th Infantry Mountain Regiment, and its first commander was Col. Onslow S. Rolfe, a cavalry officer who had to learn skiing alongside his men. The regiment spent its first winter, 1941-42, at Mount Rainier's Paradise Lodge, training on the mountain's flanks.

There the troops did things like making a winter ascent of Mount Rainier (under the guidance of Peter Gabriel) and training mules for mountain transport. Mostly, however, they concentrated on "military" skiing, working at it eight hours a day. As the Army had little previous winter-warfare experience, the troops had to improvise as they went—deciding, for instance, that the Arlberg stem-turn system was the best technique for skiing under the heavy loads that the troops would carry. The Army's lack of winter experience also led to the situation where enlisted men were teaching high-ranking officers how to ski. In the summer, at Fort Lewis, the men and mules went on conditioning trips and practiced rock climbing with ropes and pitons.

Meanwhile, in the aftermath of the Pearl Harbor attack, the Army had decided to expand the 87th to 4,000 men by the summer of 1942, and then to a full division of 15,000 men by the winter of 1943. The outfit would be known as the 10th Mountain Division; its motto, "We Climb to Conquer."

86th Infantry: Constituted Nov. 25, 1942, as the 86th Infantry. Activated Dec. 12, 1942, to May 1, 1943, at Camp Hale, Colo. Assigned to the 10th Light Division on July 15, 1943. Redesignated the 86th Mountain Infantry and assigned to the 10th Mountain Division on Nov. 6, 1944. Inactivated Nov. 27, 1945, at Camp Carson, Colo.

Questionnaire for prospective mountain troops recruits, 1943. The National Ski Patrol System served as the recruiting agency.

FH

Form 108 4.14.43

NATIONAL SKI ASSOCIATION QUESTIONNAIRE

FOR MEN SEEKING ASSIGNMENT OR TRANSFER TO MOUNTAIN TROOPS

TO: THE NATIONAL SKI PATROL SYSTEM
415 LEXINGTON AVENUE
NEW YORK CITY

I desire assignment (or transfer) to mountain troops, and I hereby apply for your assistance. If you approve my application, and there are still openings available,

A. ☐ I will ask my draft board for immediate voluntary induction, with the understanding that you will request my assignment to the Mountain Training Center when I report to my reception center, after induction. (See Instructions, Section 2)
or

B. ☐ I will wait for my regular induction, with the same understanding as above. (See instructions, Section 2)
or

C. ☐ Having already been inducted, but not having begun basic training, I apply for assignment to the Mountain Training Center for basic training. My ASN is _____, I was inducted on _____, and I have been ordered to report for active duty at _____ on (date) _____. (See Instructions, Section 2)
or

D. ☐ Having already been inducted, but undergoing basic training and still unassigned, I apply for assignment to a mountain unit upon completion of my present basic training. My ASN is _____, I was inducted on _____, and I shall complete basic training about (date) _____. (See Instructions, Section 3)
or

E. ☐ Being already in the service, and assigned, I will request transfer to mountain troops through military channels, expecting the National Ski Association to send my questionnaire to the Commanding Officer of the Mountain Training Center, for his information if my request for transfer reaches him for his approval. (See Instruction, Section 4)

I attach the required letters of recommendation.

Date _____ Applicant's Signature _____

1. NAME (Please print) _____
2. ADDRESS _____ (CITY) _____
3. AGE _____ 4. MARRIED? _____ 5. SINGLE? _____ 6. No. of DEPENDENTS _____
7. NATIVE BORN? _____ 8. NATURALIZED? _____ 9. ALIEN? _____ 10. FIRST PAPERS? _____
11. DRAFT BOARD NUMBER AND ADDRESS _____
12. INDUCTION DATE: Probable _____ Definite _____

13. EDUCATIONAL BACKGROUND (Give dates, grades and years completed)
   a. Grade School _____
   b. High School _____
   c. College _____
   d. Post Graduate and Technical _____
   e. Special Studies _____
   f. Languages Spoken and Read _____

14. PREVIOUS OCCUPATION, WITH APPROXIMATE DATES
   _____
   _____
   _____

15. HAVE YOU HAD PREVIOUS MILITARY EXPERIENCE? IF SO, DESCRIBE.

16. SKIING EXPERIENCE
   a. Cross Country _____ years, (where?) _____
   b. Downhill _____ years, (where?) _____
   c. Touring _____ years, (where?) _____
   d. Ski Mountaineering _____ years, (where?) _____
   e. No. years instructing experience _____ Professional? _____ Amateur? _____

17. MOUNTAINEERING AND CAMPING EXPERIENCE (Give locations and length of time engaged)
   a. Snow and Ice Climbing _____
   b. Rock Climbing _____
   c. Forestry Service _____
   d. Timber Cruising _____
   e. Packing horses or mules _____
   f. Mountain or forest guiding _____
   g. Trapping _____
   h. Prospecting _____

18. If you have had no skiing or mountaineering experience, write us what general qualifications for mountain training you think you have - describe camping and athletic experience, etc., and present physical condition. Use separate sheet, and attach to this sheet.

THE SATURDAY EVENING

POST

MARCH 27, 1943   10¢

RAMROD A New Western Serial By Luke Short   **WE BOMB THE U-BOAT PENS** By Lieutenant Arthur Gordon

The mountain troops gained a certain amount of notoriety with the publication of the March 1943 issue of the SATURDAY EVENING POST.

Author's collection

The pre-war ski troops. Men of the 87th Infantry Regiment, the nation's first ski troops, in training at Mount Rainier, Wash., January 1941. USA

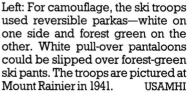

Left: For camouflage, the ski troops used reversible parkas—white on one side and forest green on the other. White pull-over pantaloons could be slipped over forest-green ski pants. The troops are pictured at Mount Rainier in 1941. USAMHI

Troops of the 87th at Mount Rainier. In the background is Paradise Lodge, which was used as a barracks.

CSM

Camp Hale, in the Eagle River Valley near Leadville, Colo., 1943. At 9,500 feet, it was the highest military camp in the United States and could house up to 10,000 troops. The camp was dismantled in the early 1950s, but some of the barracks can still be seen in the town of Leadville, about 20 miles away from the original site.

10th Mountain Div. Assoc.

A much larger training camp was needed to handle the influx of new recruits, and the Army selected a site in the Pando area of Colorado. Located 20 miles from Leadville in the Eagle River Valley, the camp was situated at 9,500 feet and was surrounded by 14,000-foot peaks—the highest Army base in the U.S. Construction on the $28 million project began in the summer of 1942 and was completed before that winter. It was named Camp Hale; to some, it would be known as "Camp Hell."

Initially, at least, there were complaints from troops about the lack of recreational facilities and weekend leave, severe discipline, and the pall of smoke that hung in the valley, spewed from passing railroad trains. Nor were the ski outings any Sunday picnic. Minnie Dole describes going out on overnight maneuvers with the troops and climbing on skis 2,800 vertical feet up Homestake Peak carrying heavily loaded packs. That night, as the men huddled in tents, the temperature dropped to minus 25. Dole writes that when he arose in the morning (after sleeping little) the camp was very quiet and he couldn't help wondering whether the men were asleep or frozen. Camp Hale was a rough place, but it did make mountain troops out of the recruits.

In August 1943, the 10th's 87th Regiment was sent to Alaska's Aleutian Islands to participate in the invasion of Japanese-held Kiska Island. After the troops had landed under the cover of a dense fog, it was discovered that the Japanese had evacuated the island several weeks previously.

In spring 1944, the entire 10th Division was moved from Camp Hale to the flat, hot plains of Camp Swift, Texas, for reasons that still are not entirely clear. During the months in Texas, the mountain troops, lacking mountains, were forced to amuse themselves however they could—climbing out of Austin hotel windows, for instance, and rappelling down to the street.

Finally, in late 1944, the 10th set sail for Europe. Its commander was Maj. Gen. George P. Hays, recipient of the Congressional Medal of Honor in World War I; its destination was northern Italy.

In Italy, the Germans had established a line of defense along the crest of the Apennines, about 35 miles north of Florence. The German positions guarded access to the Po Valley, which was highly valued by the enemy for its rich agricultural production.

HALE, COLORADO IN 1943

About 14,000 men received ski training at Camp Hale. The camp also was home to about 5,000 mules and 200 K9 dog units.   CSM

Mount Belvedere and nearby Riva Ridge were a stronghold in this defense. Three times the Fifth Army had captured this position, and three times had been driven off in counterattacks. The 10th was then given the task.

The attack has been called a classic military victory. The 10th decided to climb the heights by way of a 1,200-foot-high, nearly vertical rock face, thus hoping to surprise the Germans, who no doubt considered the face unclimbable. To prevent detection on the way up, the 10th would receive no artillery or air support.

On Feb. 18, under the cover of darkness, 800 rock-climbing soldiers started up the face. The men below were showered with rocks and earth from the men climbing above, and in places ropes had to be used to make the ascent. But the 10th surprised the Germans and took the heights. In the following days, the troops repelled numerous counterattacks, and, through bitter fighting, took other German positions on nearby mountains.

These and succeeding victories by the 10th completed the breakthrough to the Po Valley. The 10th charged ahead, overtaking one German position after another, and out running its own supply lines. On April 23, without waiting for artillery support, the 10th crossed the Po river, then chased German troops north toward the Brenner Pass.

On May 2, the action in Italy ended with the German surrender, and the 10th celebrated by holding a ski meet. The division had not used skis in any of its major actions in Italy, but its mountaineering skills were much in demand. The 10th had been responsible for crippling or destroying nine German divisions.

The division was the first to be shipped home from Europe; many of the men believed that they were to be quickly retrained and sent to help lead an attack on the Japanese mainland, but the war ended as the division arrived in the U.S. Nearly 1,000 of the 10th's men did not return, including Torger Tokle, the champion ski jumper.

The mountain troops, like any other soldiers, had to learn how to march, but skis replaced rifles during the daily workout at Camp Hale, Colo. 10th Mountain Div. Assoc.

Some of the men who arrived at Camp Hale were among the finest skiers in the world, and some had to begin with the snowplow. Pictured is a ski class, possibly on Cooper Hill, where much of the ski training took place. The ski troops found that the Arlberg stem was an effective way to turn wearing a heavy pack, and they emphasized leaning into a turn and bending the inside knee.

10th Mountain Div. Assoc.

While skis made traveling over the snow much easier, they could be a hinderance in other maneuvers, such as firing an M-1 rifle from the prone position. Training like this took place daily at Camp Hale during 1943.   10th Mountain Div. Assoc.

Ski troops learn outdoor cookery.
USAMHI

Below: Years after the war, men of the 10th get together on Minnie's Mile ski run at Vail. Another famous Vail run is Riva Ridge, named after the ridge the 10th Mountain Division conquered in Italy. A horse of the same name, owned by a Vail skier, won the Kentucky Derby.   10th Mountain Div. Assoc.

Insert: Members of the National Association of the 10th Mountain Division Inc. hold a songfest around a campfire at the 1972 Vail reunion. The association, with a membership of over 2,500, holds reunions in both the U.S. and Italy.   10th Mountain Div. Assoc.

The 10th Mountain Division was deactivated in October 1945, but it left a legacy that continues to this day—many of its veterans went on to make a lasting mark on the post-war ski industry. Pete Seibert opened Vail (where Riva Ridge has been memorialized in the name of a ski run as well as in the name of a Triple Crown winning horse owned by a Vail skier); Monty Atwater became a leading U.S. authority on avalanches; Jack Murphy opened Vermont's Sugarbush Valley; Doc DesRoches organized the Ski Industries America; Nick Hock became publisher of *Ski Business* magazine. . . . The list could go on and on. Not only did the men of the 10th Mountain Division contribute much to victory in Europe, they have contributed much to American skiing.

Opposite: Monument to the fallen comrades of the 10th Mountain Division. Located at Tennessee Pass, Colo.   10th Mountain Div. Assoc.

These photos were taken in Newfoundland, where some of the mountain troops received training in January 1943.   USA

In January 1942, the Army conducted an experiment to determine how long it would take non-skiers to gain proficiency on skis. About 150 men from Company "B," 503rd Parachute Battalion, were sent from Fort Benning, Ga., to Alta, Utah. Former racing champion Dick Durrance assembled a group of professional skiers to train the men.   USA

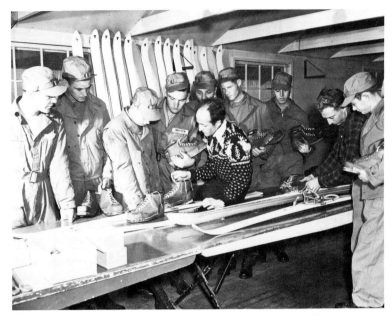

Instructors Dick Durrance (left) and Gordon Wren (right), one of America's best all-around skiers, show soldiers the proper way to fit boots to bindings.   USA

Gordon Wren teaches the herringbone method of climbing.   USA

Hugh Bauer demonstrates the kickturn, with Mount Superior in the background.   USA

Sel Hannah, a well-known racer, gives a lesson in waxing technique.   USA

During the war, skiing also was a means of recreation for many servicemen. Pictured is Norman Blanchard, formerly a California racer, at Donner Summit.   FH

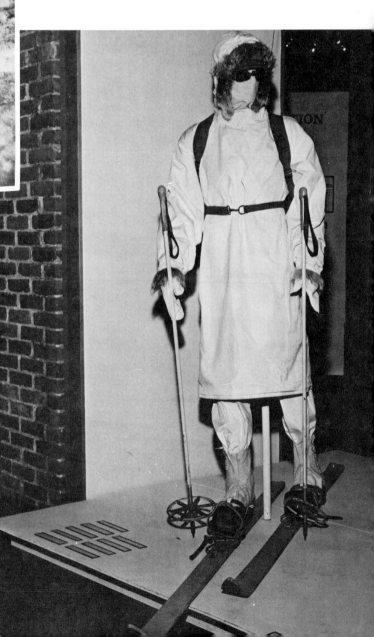

Ski-paratrooper of the 1st Special Service Force.
NESM

Winter outfit of the 1st Special Service Force. Though it was not part of the 10th Mountain Division, the force received ski instruction as well as parachute training and instruction in the use of the mechanized, over-the-snow weasel. Consisting of both American and Canadian soldiers, the force was trained at Fort Harrison near Helena, Mont., and participated in the Kiska operation and Italian campaign.   Hays Otoupalik Collection
Historical Museum at Fort Missoula (Mont.)

CHAPTER TWELVE

CELLULOID SKIING

SKI PROMOTION AND SKI MOVIES

The "Ski Lark," a New York-to-Vermont ski train, was promoted in 1949 for the opening season of Vermont's Mad River Glen. The railroads were leaders in early ski promotion.

Vermont Ski Areas Association

Since the 1930s, the sport of skiing has been heavily promoted by ski areas, equipment manufacturers, and others. Originally, when downhill skiing was first introduced to this country, Americans needed convincing that it really wasn't all that absurd to spend one's winter weekends sliding down a cold, snow-covered hill. Later, as the sport took hold, the promotion campaigns grew out of competition by ski resorts and others for the skier's dollar. Today, enormous sums are spent on ski advertising.

With the railroads' substantial resources behind them, the ski trains were among the first promoters of skiing, printing glorious color posters of the Alpine pleasures to be found in the mountainous regions serviced by their lines. Similarly, an entire state, such as New Hampshire, sometimes would be promoted for its skiing in hopes of luring city dwellers from the metropolitan areas of the East Coast.

Idaho's Sun Valley resort, built by the Union Pacific Railroad in 1936, was one of the first ski areas to be promoted on a large scale, thanks to the efforts of its master publicist, Steve Hannegan. It was no small feat to convince skiers to travel 1,000 miles to a remote and untested Idaho resort, but Hannegan was up to the task, his strategies including a poster of a shirtless male skier standing under a hot sun in addition to well-placed press releases.

As more ski areas were built in the 1930s, they too saw the value of a good publicity campaign. Holding major races was one way to establish a reputation, such as Aspen's hosting of the 1950 FIS Championships, and Squaw Valley's bid for the 1960 Winter Olympics.

The big-city ski exhibition was another means of attracting interest (and dollars) to the sport. In the 1930s, ski and sporting goods stores in New York City built borax ski slides, where customers were treated to ski demonstrations by prominent instructors. At about the same time, the Auburn Ski Club

NESM

hosted major jumping tournaments in the San Francisco Bay Area, while New York City's Madison Square Garden held an indoor ski exhibition on a mammoth 85-foot-high structure that supported a 265-foot-long ski run covered with crushed ice. During this ski show in 1936, the promoters and press invented a technique feud between Norway's Carl Messelt and Austria's Hannes Schneider, who were supposed to battle it out on the Garden's huge slide. The contest never took place, but the show was enormously successful.

As the industry matured, ski areas began to look for ways to supplement their income, which, for the most part, didn't exist in the summer months. Aspen was a leader in introducing the year-round ski resort concept by offering from its inception summertime cultural and music programs. In the last few decades, a number of other ski areas have followed suit by establishing cultural programs and institutes, and they have promoted warm-weather recreational opportunities such as fishing, hiking, riding and golf.

Skiing got another boost with the founding of nationwide publications like *SKI* (started in 1936), *Skiing,* and the more-recent *Powder* magazine. In recent years, several regional publications have appeared, including one focused on skiing in the southeastern states. These are supplemented by numerous club and ski association newsletters.

The clubs and associations also offer airline charter tours to European and Rocky Mountain resorts, while the airlines, picking up the ball from the largely discontinued snow trains, have promoted their service to mountainous areas. Despite all this, some of today's most active ski promotion is undertaken by ski equipment manufacturers, who buy countless pages of advertising.

NEW HAMPSHIRE
Land of glorious winter

A New Hampshire ski-promotion booth during the pre-war years.   NESM

A late-1930s indoor ski exhibition in San Francisco. Indoor ski shows on giant slides were popular during that decade.   FH

Ice carvings at Sun Valley's 1952 winter carnival, another form of ski promotion.   SV

"May our pages entertain and enlighten you...with humor, fashions and photographs of mountain splendors..." SKI, 1936.

Fifty years ago a young Seattle newspaperman named Alf Nydin wrote these words in a new magazine called SKI. The magazine came out at the start of the modern era of skiing and has been at the forefront of ski development ever since. It played major roles in the development of NASTAR, GLM and The Nation's Cup. In 1948 Bill Eldred combined SKI magazine, SKI NEWS, SKI ILLUSTRATED and WESTERN SKIING into today's magazine. Other American ski magazines include SKIING, POWDER and a host of regional publications.

SKI Magazine

Cover illustration for Volume 1, Number 1 of SKI, January, 1936.

OREGON'S
Timberline Lodge

Oregon's
TIMBERLINE
LODGE

MORE THAN
A MILE HIGH
ON MOUNT
HOOD'S SUNNY
SNOWFIELDS

MOUNT HOOD NATIONAL FOREST

WINTER
AT
SUN VALLEY

1940

Let's Go Skiing At
NORDEN

SUGAR BOWL   SODA SPRINGS
DONNER AREA

S·P
Southern Pacific

Colorful brochures provide ski areas with an effective
means of promotion.

Lowell Thomas, famous news broadcaster and an early advocate of skiing, made live broadcasts from various ski areas around the nation. Here he broadcasts from the Green Mountain Inn at Stowe, Vt.

SKI MOVIES

Downhill skiing and film technology both were coming of age during the 1930s, and it was during that decade that films featuring skiing began to appear with some frequency in American movie houses. Attending ski movies has since become an annual autumn ritual for many of the nation's skiers.

Making ski movies, however, is not without its problems. The sport is very "photogenic," as moviemaker John Jay describes it, but capturing skiers on film also demands that the cameraman is competent on skis. It's not surprising, then, that a number of the nation's well-known instructors and racers have made a name for themselves in the film business. Among them are Luggi Foeger, Otto Lang, Dick Durrance, Steve Bradley, and Sverre Engen. Other of the nation's top ski-movie makers include John and Lois Jay, Warren Miller, Dick Barrymore, Jim Rice, and Hans Gmoser.

The first ski film of any note was titled *The Chase,* or in German, *Der Weisse Rausch.* Filmed about 1921 by German filmmaker Dr. Arnold Fanck, it featured Rudi Matt and Hannes Schneider, who, in collaboration with Fanck, made several other ski films. These helped boost the popularity of Schneider's Arlberg technique.

In this country in the early 1930s another filmmaker and skier by the name of Christopher Young was working on a skiing spoof. Entitled *Dr. Schlitz Climbs Mt. Washington,* it was based on an incident in 1865 in which a man almost died attempting to climb New England's highest peak carrying nothing more than an umbrella. Young was helped on the project by Winston Pote, a photographer who would later document the 10th Mountain Division. The film was released in 1935 but met with only marginal financial success.

John Jay, another leading ski-movie producer, got his start in moviemaking when he was a student at St. Paul's prep school and he borrowed his family's movie camera to show why he preferred to spend his spring vacations skiing rather than returning home. After attending Williams College, he put together a ski film in 1940 entitled SKI THE AMERICAS —NORTH AND SOUTH, which included footage he had taken during college ski weekends. During World War II, which put an end to the Rhodes Scholarship he had won to Oxford, Jay served with the 10th Mountain Division, and also produced a number of training films for the military. After the war, he saw the potential of ski movies, and pursued the business full-time. Since then he has become a successful—and highly entertaining—ski-movie producer and lecturer. He still travels the world lecturing and filming. In addition, to his movies, Jay has written two books, including SKI DOWN THE YEARS, a classic ski history.   John Jay

Warren Miller is one of the world's best-known ski-movie producers. He purchased his first pair of skis (for $2) in 1936 when he was 12 years old and thereafter skied regularly. After duty with the Navy during World War II, he bought an 8-mm movie camera with his discharge pay and then moved to Sun Valley, where he filmed when he could, wrote his first book on skiing, and lived cheaply by operating out of a trailer in a parking lot and shooting rabbits for food. A very proficient racer, he eventually became a ski instructor to finance his moviemaking. His movie showings and lecture tour started in 1950, a business that grew greatly over the next three decades. NSM

Dr. Frank Howard, skiing at Alta in 1947. A pioneer in the production of ski movies, Howard was introduced to the sport on a trip to Norway in 1928. After his graduation from dental school in 1935, he acquired a movie camera and some of the latest color film and began to take movies at the Auburn Ski Club's new area in the Sierras. The popularity of the films with club members led to a lecture career in the 1930s and 1940s. Over the years he has made many ski movies, including films and publicity shots for ski areas that were just getting started, including Sun Valley and Squaw Valley. He also helped Warren Miller and John Jay in their early film careers, and he took part in the filming of the 1960 Olympics at Squaw Valley. His other skiing activities include ski racing and heading the California Ski Association. Howard now lives in San Rafael, Calif.   FH

The late 1930s saw the release of a number of ski films, and these found a better reception. One of them was *Ski Flight*, filmed in 1936 by Otto Lang and Jerome Hill at Mount Baker and Mount Rainier. The film played for six weeks at Radio City Music Hall and won a prize for "best short subject of the year." Lang, who had been an instructor at Hannes Schneider's ski school in St. Anton, also opened a ski school at Mount Rainier. Later, he would make ski-training films for the Army during World War II, and then go to Hollywood as a film producer.

In the late 1930s a number of ski-chase movies were made, inspired by Fanck's original. For instance, Dick Durrance and Steve Bradley used the new resort at Ketchum, Idaho, as the setting for their 1940 film entitled *Sun Valley Ski Chase*.

The color and sound ski films that began to appear about this time were in many respects pioneered by Dr. Frank Howard, a ski racer and practicing dentist living in Caifornia. Howard first experimented with color in the mid-1930s right after his graduation from dental school, and in 1935 put together his first amateur film on skiing, shot at the Auburn Ski Club. The club's reaction to the first showing was so good that it started Howard on a career in filmmaking which would last many years and would include films featuring the top names in skiing, the top ski areas, and films made for many corporate clients.

In the East, a young Harvard graduate by the name of Sidney Shurcliff made several well-received ski films just before World War II, and these, in turn, helped inspire John Jay, a recent Williams College graduate, to enter the ski-movie business with a 1940 film titled *Ski the Americas—North and South.*

After the war, a number of ski-film makers, among them John Jay and Warren Miller, released films on a regular basis. Hollywood also got into the act with feature-length films either about skiing or set in ski resorts. Perhaps the most famous of these is the 1940 *Sun Valley Serenade,* starring John Payne and the famous Olympic skater Sonja Henie. More recently, skiing has been featured in such films as *Downhill Racer* (1969), starring Robert Redford and Gene Hackman, as well as two James Bond movies, *On Her Majesty's Secret Service* and *For Your Eyes Only.* The latter offers a thrilling ski-with-machine-gun chase sequence down a terrifying Alpine obstacle course which ends in mid-air.

SUN VALLEY SERENADE, a film from 20th Century-Fox, 1940.
Academy of Motion Picture
Arts & Sciences

John Payne, one of the actors in
SUN VALLEY SERENADE.
  Academy of Motion Picture
  Arts & Sciences

DOWNHILL RACER, from Para-
mount Pictures, 1969.
  Academy of Motion Picture
  Arts & Sciences

CHAPTER THIRTEEN

ALL THAT GLITTERS

THE BIRTH OF SUN VALLEY,
AMERICA'S FIRST MAJOR SKI RESORT

Sun Valley's Challenger Inn, 1941.   SV

For weeks during the winter of 1935-36, Austrian Count Felix Schaffgotsch had been combing the American West in search of the perfect place for a major American ski resort, to be built by the Union Pacific Railroad. Hired by his friend, UP Board Chairman Averell Harriman, Schaffgotsch had finally arrived in a little Idaho ranching town called Ketchum.

He liked the place, lying as it did near the foot of the Sawtooth Mountains and blessed with a nice climate and dry snow, and he set off around the valley on skis to find the ideal spot to build a lodge—a spot where the sun shone long and bright and where the air currents were warmest.

Schaffgotsch was out exploring the valley one day when he ran into Roberta Brass Garretson, whose father owned a local ranch. The count told the woman what he was doing.

"I laughed," recalled Mrs. Garretson in Oppenheimer and Poore's book *Sun Valley,* "and I said, 'you know, when the weather gets cold, I always notice the stock going to this particular spot.' "

"Schaffgotsch asked where that spot might be," continue the authors of *Sun Valley,* "since naturally, if the cows were huddling there on cold days, it must have meant that was the warmest place in the valley. Roberta pointed out the area, and Schaffgotsch bowed, saying, 'That is the area I selected.' "

Thus did Count Schaffgotsch receive bovine confirmation of his selection of a lodge site. It marked the end of a search that had taken him all over the American West, and it marked the beginning of a new concept in American skiing— the full-scale winter sports resort, built from the ground up and modeled after the famous European Alpine resorts. Many more of these built-from-scratch American resorts would follow— Vail, Jackson Hole, Snowmass, and others—but Sun Valley was, and remains, the original.

Felix Schaffgotsch, the Austrian count who chose the location for America's first full-scale ski resort.
SV

For years Sun Valley set the standard for American ski resorts, and for years it was a haven for Hollywood stars, society people, European royalty, and powerful American businessmen. It offered the best in luxurious living and a wide assortment of sports, not to mention the world's first chairlift. In short, Sun Valley, a former cow and sheep pasture, became a symbol of all that glittered in American skiing.

This transformation from pastureland to major resort did indeed happen almost overnight—it was only about one year from Count Schaffgotsch's first visit until the resort's opening. But the birth of Sun Valley, unlike previous American resorts that had been built up bit by bit, also required an enormous chunk of money, precise planning, and a brilliantly effective publicity campaign.

Behind it all was Averell Harriman, in his mid-40s at the time, who had worked his way up through the ranks of the railroad that his father had taken over in the 1890s. Harriman had been to Europe and realized how popular skiing vacations were among the bankers and business executives he called upon, and he decided that a major ski resort might be a way to increase passenger traffic on the UP's lines, many of which served snowbound areas such as Colorado, Idaho, Utah, and Wyoming. At the same time, he figured, a major ski resort would be a boon to the people of the state in which it was built.

Thus he hired Felix Schaffgotsch, who knew his way around European ski resorts, gave the count the help of the Union Pacific's personnel, and asked him to explore the American West.

Schaffgotsch's search was not any easy one. He tried Mount Rainier, but rejected it because it was on public land; he checked out Mount Hood, but the pouring rain on the day of his arrival put him off; Yosemite, too, was public land; he looked at Aspen, but at about 8,000 feet the town was too high (the Europeans tried to keep their resorts under 6,000 feet, concerned that the altitude would affect their guests' health); Alta had good skiing, but was too close to Salt Lake City; Jackson Hole came close, but the Wyoming highway department couldn't guarantee to keep the pass open in winter.

After checking out a few places in Idaho (and rejecting them), Count Schaffgotsch, frustrated, returned to Colorado, where he planned to look at one more area and thereafter return to New York, where he expected he'd have to tell Harriman that he'd failed in his search.

Schaffgotsch had left word with UP's Idaho-area representative, William Hynes, to wire him in Denver if Hynes had any more ideas about a ski-area location. One evening not long after the count's departure for Denver, Hynes, who had squired Schaffgotsch all over Idaho and Wyoming on the search, was having a drink with a friend, Idaho's director of highways, Joe Simmer. Hynes told Simmer about the count's fruitless search. According to an account in the book *Sun Valley,* Simmer then asked, "Did you look in the Hailey and Ketchum area?" "By God no," Hynes replied. "I forgot."

The count was summoned. He arrived in Ketchum under clear blue, windless skies, and he began to see the possibility of the place. Ketchum at that time was a former mining boom town, which, since the bottom dropped out of the silver market in the 1890s, had dwindled to a population of 270, many of them cattle and sheep ranchers.

As Schaffgotsch began his explorations around the valley on skis, word spread through the tiny town that an Austrian count was looking for a place to build a large ski resort. This bit of news prompted the now-legendary response of one local sheep rancher: "Be nice to him, but don't cash any of his checks."

Then Averell Harriman showed up in his private railroad car. Schaffgotsch had wired Harriman that the area "contains more delightful features than any other place I have seen in the U.S., Switzerland, or Austria for a winter sports center." These features, in the count's mind, included dry powder, largely windless conditions, good-sized mountains, the proper altitude, and lots of sun.

The UP board went along with Board Chairman Harriman's plan to build a resort, and the railroad purchased ranchland near Ketchum, including land belonging to the Brass family. Yet Harriman realized that a strong publicity campaign would be vital to the success of a resort that would be built essentially in the middle of nowhere and that would feature what to most Americans was a largely unknown sport. Thus he hired Steve Hannegan, the man who had promoted Miami Beach. Hannegan had no love for winter weather.

According to Ezra Bowen's *American Skiing,* Hannegan traveled to Ketchum, arriving in a covered handcar, and looked around: "All I could see was a goddam field of snow. I thought they must be crazy. 'This is strictly ridiculous,' I said. But we walked around some more, with my shoes full of snow, and then the sun came out. It began to feel pretty good, so I opened my coat. Then I took it off. Pretty soon I opened my vest. Then I began to sweat . . . " The name "Sun Valley" came into being.

Originally, Averell Harriman had planned to build a rather small lodge at the site, "and see how it would work." But Hannegan had other ideas. Figuring it should be done in a big way or not at all, he envisioned a first-class hotel, an ice rink, outdoor swimming pool, billiard parlor, bowling alley and movie theater, plus ski lifts and a very selective reservation list.

In the spring of 1936, ground was broken for the Sun Valley Lodge, a building that would be constructed of concrete (for longevity and fire prevention) poured into forms made of pine boards that would leave their grain imprinted on the hardened concrete. The structure, anything but a small lodge, would have room for 288 guests and 124 employees.

Meanwhile, out in the flatlands at UP's Omaha headquarters, railroad engineers were trying to figure out how to transport skiers up Sun Valley's mountains. The engineers considered a J-bar, an uphill toboggan, a cable car, and other devices in use at other ski areas. Then an engineer by the name of Jim Curran came up with something totally new. Before joining UP, he had worked on designing a conveyor system, using cables and hooks, to load bananas on South American fruit boats. He wondered if the hooks holding bananas could be replaced with chairs holding skiers. The chairlift was born.

Sun Valley opened on Dec. 21, 1936, sporting the new lodge and chairlifts on two rather small mountains, Dollar and Proctor. Steve Hannegan's public relations work had brought in society folk and Hollywood stars, including Sam Goldwyn, Tommy Hitchcock, Robert Young, and Claudette Colbert. The lodge, standing like a bastion of luxury in the midst of the Idaho wilderness, provided an opening banquet that night with a menu that included Manhattan cocktail, brioche au caviar, supremes of sole au champagne valley lodge, tournedos sautes chatelaine, and many other dishes, while after dinner the guests danced to Harl Smith's band, imported from New York City.

Two Sun Valley kingpins keep an eye on construction, 1936. Averell Harriman (left), board chairman of the Union Pacific Railroad, came up with the idea to build the resort; Steve Hannegan (right) came up with the promotional wizardry that put it on the map.   SV

Dollar Mountain, smallest of Sun Valley's ski mountains and site of the world's first chairlift, constructed in 1936. It took a few tries to get used to the thing, but soon chairlifts were under construction all across the country. SV

Everything was going according to plan, but for one problem. Sun Valley had no snow.

A couple of inches covered the valley, leftovers from a mid-December storm, but nowhere near enough to ski. For recreation, guests had to make do with card games, ping pong, outdoor swimming, and bus trips to the top of a nearby pass where one could find enough snow to ski. It all began to seem like a long, rainy day at summer camp, where counselors worked frantically to keep their wards busy and happy.

On Dec. 27, it snowed five inches, but the resort had neglected to cut down the sagebrush on the ski slopes at Dollar and Proctor. The stubble protruded through the thin cover—still no skiing, and the guests were given free room and board until there was.

New Year's Eve was Sun Valley's second big party, and it brought a new influx of Hollywood types, among them Errol Flynn and Joan Bennett. Other Hollywood people were with the crew of *I Met Him in Paris*, which had come to Sun Valley to shoot the film's winter sports sequences.

On New Year's Eve it finally snowed—nearly two feet this time—but Sun Valley's real publicity triumph that night came from an unplanned, and unpleasant, incident that occurred during the party. Investment banker C.F. Glore apparently asked Claudette Colbert to dance, but somebody (news reports said it was movie producer David O. Selznick, while a witness says it was Errol Flynn) objected to the invitation and punched Glore. The next day, the *New York Herald Tribune* ran a story with the headline, "Sun Valley Opens With A Bang."

The resort was off and running, although it was far from profitable. Much of its success was due to the promotion efforts of Steve Hannegan, who came up with the idea for the famous publicity photo of a young man, stripped to the waist, standing on a pair of skis under a hot sun. Other events that carried the name Sun Valley throughout the world were the filming of *Sun Valley Serenade,* and the arrival of Ernest Hemingway, who first visited the area in the late 1930s and who eventually established a home there.

One of Steve Hannegan's promotional strokes of genius. A model was smeared with Vaseline and posed in a New York studio on cotton gauze that was make to look like snow. The result supposedly portrayed typical Sun Valley weather, and the photo was used on the resort's first ski poster.   SV

The opening of Baldy Mountain in the late 1930s greatly expanded the area's potential. Pictured is Baldy's famous Roundhouse restaurant, located partway up the mountain. 1947.   SV

1937

In early 1936, Sun Valley was a pasture in the middle of the Idaho wilderness. By 1937 (top), it was a luxury resort in the middle of the Idaho wilderness, with ice rink, outdoor swimming pool, and ski slopes. By the 1960s (bottom), Sun Valley had grown considerably, and its reputation had long since been secured.   SV

The core of the Sun Valley facilities. Top: Sun Valley Lodge, the first of the resort's accommodations. Middle: The lodge, with heated outdoor swimming pool in foreground. Bottom: The ski school meeting place and the Challenger Inn, built after the resort's opening and offering accommodations that were less expensive than those of the main lodge and were intended for a younger crowd.   SV

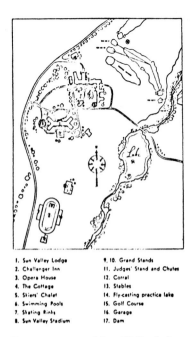

Pre-war map of Sun Valley's base facilities. The last four decades have seen tremendous growth here, including the addition of many apartment and condominium units.　　　　SV

1. Sun Valley Lodge
2. Challenger Inn
3. Opera House
4. The Cottage
5. Skiers' Chalet
6. Swimming Pools
7. Skating Rinks
8. Sun Valley Stadium
9. 10. Grand Stands
11. Judges' Stand and Chutes
12. Corral
13. Stables
14. Fly-casting practice lake
15. Golf Course
16. Garage
17. Dam

By today's standards, rates at the Challenger Inn were incredibly low; by Sun Valley standards, they were low, too. Suites in the main lodge started at $48 per night.　　SV

Yet, all the luxury and glitter aside, the skiing itself during the early years of Sun Valley wasn't all that good. Baldy, the large mountain that looms over Ketchum, had not yet been developed. In about 1939, however, Averell Harriman decided to build a chair on Baldy. Working against the deadline imposed by the season's first snows, engineers and laborers built the chair by working both from the top down (where the snow would fall first) and from the bottom up. The lift was completed on time and under budget, and the extra funds were used to build the octagon-shaped Roundhouse restaurant partway up the mountain.

With the opening of Baldy, Sun Valley had itself a real skiers' mountain. It became host to the most important event on the American racing circuit—the Harriman Cup (which was discontinued in 1965), named after Averell Harriman, who donated the large silver bowl. Harriman was a strong believer in competition, and his resort helped develop more than its share of great racers—among them Gretchen Fraser, Clarita Heath, Barney McLean and Ernie McCullough.

Baldy's good skiing, and Sun Valley's policy of giving its employees a free ski pass, also helped create a new sub-class of American society—the ski bum. Warren Miller, for example, spent a winter in a trailer at the base of Baldy. Later he went on to produce a number of ski films. Ed Scott came out to Sun Valley as a well-educated ski bum. Then he started his own ski pole factory.

The years from 1937 to 1941 were the glamour years at Sun Valley; when war broke out the resort became a Navy hospital, and after the war things began to change. By about 1950 Averell Harriman had gone into politics, and the UP had a new president who became concerned about the losses the railroad was taking at Sun Valley. In its early years, the resort had bestowed all sorts of gifts upon its favored guests, but it now became more budget-minded, as did its clientele.

By 1964, it was clear that the resort needed work, and Union Pacific hired the Janss Corp., which had been involved with the development of Snowmass, to study Sun Valley's facilities. The Janss team believed that $5 million would have to be spent on the resort, but the railroad was not prepared to make that sort of commitment. Sun Valley was then sold to the Janss Corp. for $3 million.

Bill Janss, a former racer who had been named to the 1940 Olympic team and the son of a California developer, saw Sun Valley's potential as a year-round resort rather than simply as a winter sports center. Under the Janss Corp., Sun Valley put in millions of dollars in improvements—remodeling the lodge, new tennis courts, new swimming pool, improved golf course, skeet shooting, and other recreational facilities. And there has been condominium construction that has helped boost the area's number of beds considerably. Some have objected to the expansion of Sun Valley, but, compared to many other resorts, Sun Valley is still relatively small.

Perhaps most important, the Janss Corp. went to work on Baldy. Only two lifts had been built since 1939, but under the new ownership, with former racer Janss seeing the attraction of skiing the steep, Sun Valley developed the long, steep Warm Springs side of the mountain.

In 1977, Sun Valley changed hands again. It is now part of the Little America chain of hotels, under the ownership of R. Earl Holding.

Sun Valley isn't quite the glamour spot it was in its early days—it seems to be more family-oriented now—but the visitor still might spot the occasional movie star sitting at the next table. The luxury is still there for those willing to pay, although there are alternatives for those who are not. As for the skiing, which is the reason this dreamland was built out of a pasture in the first place: despite a big chunk of intermediate terrain, Baldy is a hard-core skiers' mountain, one of the finest to be found in the United States. When it comes to major American ski resorts, Sun Valley is still near the top of the list.

Sun Valley became a haven for Hollywood celebrities and society people. Many of them actually skied. Here, Sigi Engl, head of the ski school, coaches Gary Cooper and Clark Gable. SV

Other movie people visiting Sun Valley were Dick Powell and June Allyson, pictured here. Some, such as Darryl Zanuck, Norma Shearer and Ann Southern, spent considerable time at the resort. The valley's most famous resident, however, was not a Hollywood star, but a writer—Ernest Hemingway, who would end his life here in 1961. SV

In addition to the movie moguls, Sun Valley drew some of the world's best skiers. Stein Eriksen, Sigi Engl and Christian Pravda carve through the dry Idaho snow, 1953. SV

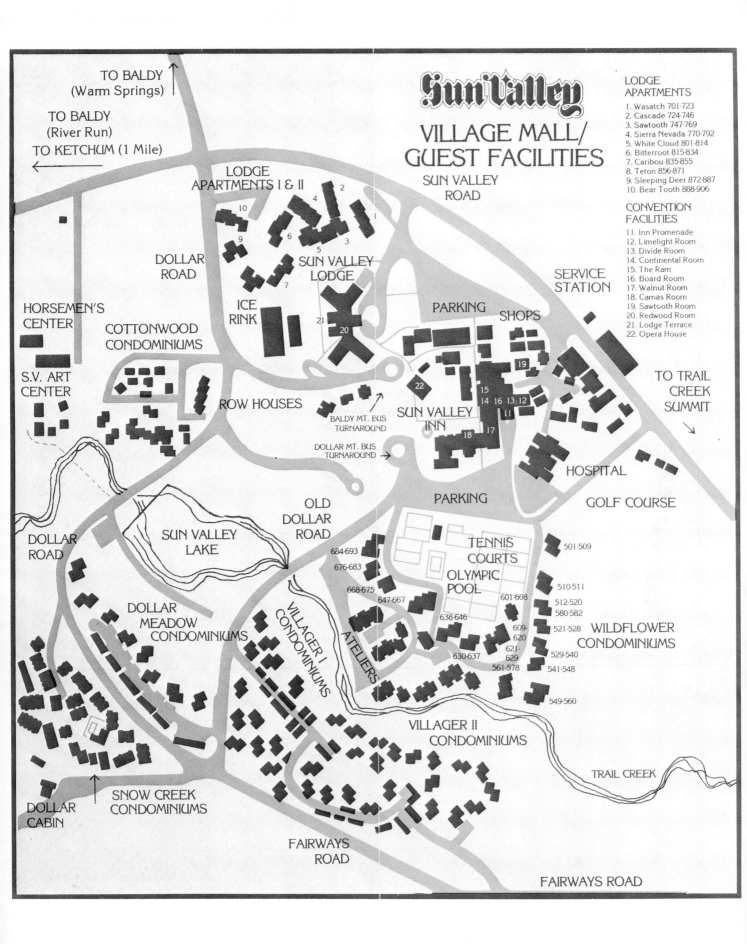

TO BALDY
(Warm Springs)

TO BALDY
(River Run)

TO KETCHUM (1 Mile)

Sun Valley

VILLAGE MALL/
GUEST FACILITIES

SUN VALLEY
ROAD

LODGE
APARTMENTS I & II

DOLLAR
ROAD

SUN VALLEY
LODGE

HORSEMEN'S
CENTER

COTTONWOOD
CONDOMINIUMS

ICE
RINK

SERVICE
STATION

PARKING

SHOPS

S.V. ART
CENTER

ROW HOUSES

BALDY MT. BUS
TURNAROUND

SUN VALLEY
INN

TO TRAIL
CREEK
SUMMIT

DOLLAR MT. BUS
TURNAROUND

HOSPITAL

OLD
DOLLAR
ROAD

PARKING

GOLF COURSE

DOLLAR
ROAD

SUN VALLEY
LAKE

TENNIS
COURTS

OLYMPIC
POOL

684-693

676-683

668-675

647-667

638-646

601-608

609-620

621-629

630-637

561-578

501-509

510-511

512-520

580-582

521-528

529-540

541-548

549-560

WILDFLOWER
CONDOMINIUMS

DOLLAR
MEADOW
CONDOMINIUMS

VILLAGER I
CONDOMINIUMS

ATELIERS

VILLAGER II
CONDOMINIUMS

TRAIL CREEK

DOLLAR
CABIN

SNOW CREEK
CONDOMINIUMS

FAIRWAYS
ROAD

FAIRWAYS ROAD

Courtesy Sun Valley

CHAPTER FOURTEEN

RAGS TO RICHES

OLD MINING TOWNS FIND SILVER IN THE SNOW

Aspen, 1947.   DPL

In 1800, much of America's Rocky Mountain region was an unexplored, uncharted mountain kingdom. The first few decades of the 19th century brought explorers and fur trappers, and the latter part of the century saw the region come alive with the discovery of gold and silver, drawing hordes of stampeding prospectors from the East.

The early mining towns were some of the first settlements in the high-mountain areas of Colorado, Idaho, Utah, and Montana. Those located near rich ore bodies flourished. Some had thousands of inhabitants, and dozens of hotels and saloons, as well as opera houses, railroad sidings and no lack of nightlife. Then, in 1893 Congress repealed the Sherman Silver Act. Silver was demonitized, its price plummeted, and many of the Rocky Mountain mining towns became "ghosted," their inhabitants departing for greener pastures or new mineral strikes such as those in the distant Yukon.

Other towns barely hung on, their residents turning to ranching, logging, and other activities. These communities would lie dormant until World War II. At that point skiers discovered the sleepy little mountain towns, and with the skiers came a second boom.

In many ways, the towns were ideal for skiing—they were situated at high elevations, they were surrounded by tall, skiable mountains, and they were blessed with prodigious quantities of snow. And they had "atmosphere." Where the European ski resorts took their flavor from ancient, pastoral Alpine farming villages, the Rocky Mountain ski towns possessed the look and atmosphere of the early mining days, a flavor that was at once properly Victorian as well as wild and wide-open.

Some of these towns have since become legends in the world of skiing; others are less well known, but are patronized by hard-core devotees. These former mining towns include Aspen, Alta, Breckenridge, Park City, Red Lodge, and Telluride, four of which are discussed here.

ASPEN

Aspen was originally called "Ute City," after the Indians who possessed lands in the area. The first white settlers, silver prospectors who arrived in the late 1870s, were driven away by fear of Indian raids. By the early 1880s, however, the miners had returned and laid out a town, renaming it "Aspen."

During that decade, Aspen became one of the West's largest silver centers, with a total of over $120 million worth of silver being produced during the next 70 years. At its peak, in the early 1890s, the town boasted almost 12,000 inhabitants, in addition to a hospital, several hotels, a courthouse, 10 churches, three banks, two railroads, and six newspapers. But the collapse of the silver market hit Aspen hard. By the 1930s the town was dependent on farming and ranching, and only about 600 inhabitants remained. It is said that not a single new house was built in Aspen in the 40 years preceeding the end of World War II.

After Sun Valley had been constructed in Idaho in 1936, investors began to look at Aspen with the same idea. (Sun Valley's founders had considered Aspen as a possible site for their resort, but rejected it because of its high elevation.) In the late 1930s, federal WPA workers built a short "boat tow" up Aspen (or Ajax) Mountain, and local skiers helped cut a run on the mountain's face, naming it in honor of prominent Swiss skier Andre Roch, who did much to bring skiing to Aspen in the pre-war years. Meanwhile, in nearby Ashcroft, the beginnings of a ski area were established on the huge Mount Hayden, but World War II interrupted these projects.

During the war, the 10th Mountain Division was based not far from Aspen at Camp Hale, and the sleepy little town with the big mountain caught the eye of some of the ski troops. Among them was Friedl Pfeifer.

Returning to Aspen after the war, Pfeifer met up with Walter Paepcke, who was chairman of the Container Corporation of America and who was looking for a place to build a summer cultural center. Thus was born a resort that offered cultural opportunities during the summer and skiing during the winter.

Aspen's first chairlift opened in 1947 on Aspen Mountain. The first years were tough. The few runs that Aspen did offer were mostly too difficult for the average skier, and the mountain also contained some difficult obstacles—open mineshafts, for instance.

Aspen about 1946, just before the town would become a major U.S. ski resort. The town has grown immensely since this photo was taken.
FH

Opposite: Early skiers in the Aspen area. The miners and settlers in the early mining towns used "snow-shoes" for transportation and sometimes for racing.
Aspen Historical Society

In 1950, Aspen managed to attract the FIS World Championships. This event, along with a very successful summer cultural program celebrating Goethe's Bicentennial, put Aspen on the international map.

From there the place took off and hasn't stopped yet, although in recent years growth has been curtailed somewhat by environmental concerns. In the late 1950s, another mountain, Aspen Highlands, opened for skiing, and a few years later, Buttermilk, an area aimed at beginners, opened just down the road. Meanwhile, the town grew with hotels, lodges, houses, restaurants, and condominiums. Real estate prices skyrocketed, and Aspen became a world-class resort.

In the late 1960s, the Snowmass ski resort opened a few miles from Aspen. A self-contained village and ski area, the project initially was spearheaded by Bill Janss, later the owner of Sun Valley. The mountain has been developed considerably over the years, and now is one of the largest ski areas in the United States, with more annual skier-days than Aspen's three other mountains combined.

Skiing in Aspen in 1939. In the late 1930s, the WPA built a boat tow part way up Aspen Mountain, but a full-scale ski area was not developed there until after the war.
DPL

Aspen's famous ski school. Friedl Pfeifer, one of the founders of the ski area at Aspen, co-directed the school with Fred Iselin.
Author's collection

Aspen's Mill Street about 1950, when the ski resort was just getting on its feet. On the right is the landmark Wheeler Opera House, built in 1889.   NA

Aspen hosted the 1950 FIS World Championships, an event that did much to establish its reputation in the skiing world.   FH

The Sundeck restaurant on top of Aspen (or Ajax) Mountain, 1950.
DPL, Charles Grover photo

Aspen's first chairlift opened on Aspen Mountain in January 1947. The chair, said to be the world's longest, carried skiers over this old house, a relic of Aspen's glorious silver-mining days.
FH

ALTA

Alta has a history similar to Aspen's, although Alta has always been a much smaller settlement. Tucked away in Little Cottonwood Canyon near Salt Lake City, Alta may not feature a big, bustling ski town like Aspen, but it does offer some of the world's finest powder skiing as well as some very tough runs.

Moving from the East in the 1840s, Mormons settled the wilderness that then surrounded the Great Salt Lake. Within two decades of their arrival, a rich silver vein was discovered at Emma Hill, near the site of present-day Alta. By 1873, Alta was a substantial town, with 180 buildings and a population of nearly 3,000. The area's silver production during the 1870s totaled about $13.5 million.

Mining slackened during the last two decades of the 19th century and Alta was hit with avalanches that devastated the community and claimed dozens of lives, but the area experienced a second and very brief mining boom during the late teens. By the early 1930s, however, Alta possessed only a handful of inhabitants.

One of its few stalwarts was George H. Watson, who had come from the East around 1900 with the idea of entering the mining business. Over the years, Watson had acquired many mining properties in the area. He had also been dubbed "mayor" of Alta.

In the late 1930s, a group of Salt Lake City skiers and businessmen, inspired by the example of Sun Valley, began to look at Alta as the site for a ski resort. George Watson, either in trouble with his creditors or taken with the dream of building a ski area, or both (accounts differ), donated 1,800 acres of land to the U.S. Forest Service so the area could be built.

The first chairlift at Alta opened in 1938. Constructed in part from old ore-bucket conveyors, it hauled skiers up a hefty 2,630 vertical feet for 15 cents per ride. Soon a few buildings were constructed at the base, including the Alta Lodge, financed in part by the Denver and Rio Grande Railroad. Meanwhile, George Watson had set himself up as a sort of one-man welcoming committee for visitors and skiers, operating out of a snow-covered cabin that was accessible by ladder, where he served exotic drinks flavored with items like pine needles. Another of Alta's early supporters was James Laughlin, head of New Directions Press.

Alta's ski school was headed in the early years first by Karl Fahrner and later by Dick Durrance, who eventually would move to Aspen. During World War II, Durrance assembled some of America's finest skiers to train soldiers at Alta. This was part of an experiment to determine how long it would take to teach non-skiing soldiers (in this case paratroopers) how to ski. Hundreds of other troops stationed in the region also came to Alta for recreational skiing.

At the end of the war, Alta had three lifts and two lodges. In the years after the war, Alta grew with the addition of more lifts, several new lodges, and then condominiums and houses. Like many ski resorts, Alta eventually underwent a development fight as residents tried to determine just how large a community it should be.

The ski school grew also, flourishing under the leadership of well-known jumper and racer Alf Engen, while Alta's avalanche control personnel, such as Monty Atwater and Ed LaChapelle, pioneered many techniques to keep the mountain safe—among them the use of artillery to shoot down unstable slopes. Other ski areas were also built nearby. Snowbird, for instance, is just a mile down the road.

In the beginning, Alta's founders didn't intend to build a "destination" resort; their aim was to attract a local crowd, and Alta is still a small resort compared to an Aspen or a Vail. Through the years, however, Alta's famous powder and its challenging slopes have drawn skiers from the world over as well as those from nearby Salt Lake.

Figure-eights down Alta's Rustler Mountain. The area is famous for its deep powder.
Utah State Historical Society

Alta, Utah, as it appeared in 1873, near the height of its mining days. Like many of the West's mining towns, it declined in the late 19th century when the silver market fell off, but Alta came back to life in the late 1930s with the construction of a major ski resort.
WASM

Speaker system used in Alta's early days. The speakers broadcasted warnings of avalanche danger on the south slopes above Snowline Lodge. Alta has pioneered a number of avalanche control techniques, such as shooting down unstable slopes with artillery.
Utah State Historical Society

Upper Collins Gulch at Alta, showing the Watson shelter and lift terminal, 1941.   USFS

Rustler Mountain, 1941.   USFS

Upper terminal of Alta's Germania
lift, 1956.   USFS

PARK CITY

The idea for a ski resort at Park City was born in the mid-1930s, at about the same time Aspen and Alta were first being considered for skiing. But, unlike Aspen and Alta, Park City would wait many years for a major lift.

The Park City area, not far from Salt Lake City, was first explored in the 1840s by Mormons and was settled in the 1860s and 1870s by silver miners. Some of the prospectors came from Alta after that area had been completely claimed. By 1879, Park City had 350 buildings; 15 year later, like other silver-mining towns, it was in the grip of a depression. In Park City's case this was exacerbated by a major fire in 1898 which destroyed a large chunk of the town.

Park City remained a mining town, however, and it hosted its first ski tournament in 1923 when a group of ski jumpers arrived from Salt Lake City. Jumping tournaments were held sporadically thereafter, and in the mid-1930s, when the town was floundering in the Great Depression, a WPA official suggested constructing a major ski resort. The citizens agreed, and some construction and some skiing started immediately, but the momentum was lost during World War II as local metal mining underwent a resurgence.

After the war, there were other attempts to establish a ski resort at Park City, such as the T-bar that was built in 1946, but none of these resulted in large-scale construction. In the meantime, the mining industry fell off again, and the area continued to lose population.

About 1960, Park City was officialy designated a "depressed area" by the federal government, which qualified it for low-interest loans. This helped convince the United Park City Mines Co. to develop a ski area, as the company was looking for a way to diversify. Sporting a two-mile-long gondola, the area opened in December 1963. With other developments nearby, Park City has since become one of the nation's major ski areas.

The past blends with the present at the old mining town of Park City, located near Salt Lake City, Utah.
Park City Ski Corp.

TELLURIDE

Telluride is one of America's newest ski resorts. Small in comparison to other resorts, it contains relatively few large-scale modern buildings, and has managed to preserve much of the flavor (as well as the architecture) of its early mining days. As such, Telluride has proven attractive to skiers who wish to escape the sprawling growth of some of the other Colorado ski resorts.

Situated at the end of a spectacular box canyon and flanked by high cliffs, Telluride got its start in the 1870s when prospectors found gold and silver. Its name probably was derived from tellurium, a gold-bearing ore, although one legend maintains that the name means "to Hell you ride," a reference to the boisterous nature of the early mining town.

By the early 1900s, Telluride counted about 5,000 inhabitants and had been the scene both for a bank holdup by Butch Cassidy and for a famous speech delivered by William Jennings Bryan. Downhill skiing arrived in the 1930s when residents constructed a primitive rope tow and local skiers competed against teams from other Colorado communities.

The drive for a full-scale ski area was initiated by Billy Mahoney, who had moved to Telluride with his family in the early 1930s and became a top local racer. After serving with the Navy during World War II, Mahoney built a portable rope tow out of a 1934 Nash Rambler that could be set up wherever the snow happened to be best.

In the late 1940s, Mahoney was turned down by the Forest Service for a ski area permit. In the early 1960s he and other local residents formed a ski corporation, but this was later dissolved due to financial problems. The long-sought ski area finally got underway in the late 1960s with the backing of Joseph Zoline, a California industrialist who had moved to Aspen and then to Telluride. Mahoney was named mountain manager of the new ski area, and almost single-handedly constructed the mountain's first ski trails.

Telluride opened in 1972 and now has 24 miles of trail, six lifts, and a substantial 3,100 feet of vertical drop. The town, which was designated a National Historical Landmark in 1964, is billed in promotional literature as the "City of Gold," while the mountain is called the "Mountain of White Gold."

CHAPTER FIFTEEN

SKIING SOUTHERN STYLE

North Carolina's largest ski area is Sugar Mountain, located near Banner Elk. The runs drop 1,200 feet from a 5,300-foot summit.   North Carolina High Country Host

Until recently, when a skier thought of the South—if he thought of it at all—any hopes of skiing most likely were overpowered by images of fried chicken, mint juleps, and tangled swamps. The closest thing to snow, he imagined, were cotton fields covering the steamy flatlands, and the nearest skiable mountain he no doubt placed several hundred miles west of the Mississippi.

Since about 1960 this skier's image of the South has changed. The mountains have always been there—thousands of square miles of them, including North Carolina's Mount Mitchell, at 6,684 feet the highest mountain in the East. But what the South lacked was a reliable snowfall. With the invention of snowmaking equipment, however, Southern skiing came into its own.

The South, of course, lagged far behind the rest of the U.S. in the development of ski areas. The great boom in ski area construction that followed World War II quite naturally bypassed the South; the action was where the snow fell—New England, the West, the Midwest. Through the 1940s, the 1950s, and the early 1960s, Southern resorts continued to promote their sunshine and their retirement homes.

The first sign of change came in the 1950s when the Washington (D.C.) Ski Club built a little ski area in the Potomac Highlands, in a sparsely populated area of Tucker County, W.Va., about 150 miles west of the nation's capital. Weiss Knob, as the hill was known, had no snowmaking and probably appealed only to federal employees who had been transferred to Washington from snow states and who refused to give up their love of skiing. Weiss Knob did, however, introduce the idea that skiing in the South was feasible.

Weiss Knob in Tucker County, W.Va., during the 1950s. The Washington (D.C.) Ski Club developed this small area, one of the first in the South. In the last few years, several large resorts—such as Mount Timberline and Canaan Valley—have been developed in Tucker County.

State of West Virginia

In 1958, an Austrian by the name of Sepp Kober arrived at Weiss Knob by way of Stowe, Vt. A former member of the German Alpine Troops, Kober had become prominent in European ski circles and had directed ski schools and coached the Norwegian and Spanish ski teams. He would come to be known as "the father of Southern skiing."

Kober's stay at Weiss Knob was brief, but apparently it convinced him of the feasibilty of skiing in the South, for in the spring of 1959 he arrived at The Homestead, the world-famous health spa and resort tucked away in the rugged mountains of Bath County, Va. There Kober proceeded to build the South's first real ski area.

Starting with an old golf course, Kober laid out trails, installed snowmaking equipment (which by then was advanced enough to allow 100 percent coverage of The Homestead's slopes), and built a trestle lift system similar to the one in use at North Conway, N.H. The opening of The Homestead's slopes in December 1959 marked the beginning of a boom in Southern skiing.

The South's first full-fledged ski area opened in the late 1950s at The Homestead, the internationally known resort and health spa located in the Blue Ridge Mountains of Bath County, Va. This trestle, similar to the one at Cranmore Mountain, N.H., was built in 1959; the slope formerly was part of a golf course.   The Homestead

The Homestead's trestle was replaced in 1980 by this chairlift. Improvements in snowmaking equipment in the 1950s paved the way for development of Southern ski areas that, like The Homestead, were located in regions of moderate snowfall.

The Homestead

Sepp Kober, "the father of Southern skiing" and developer of The Homestead's ski area, pictured with friends in front of the resort's main building. The resort's history as a health spa dates back to the 1760s.

The Homestead

Appalachian Ski Mountain at Blowing Rock, N.C.   North Carolina High Country Host

Ski area developers first concentrated on the high-elevation, cold-temperature areas of the Upper South. A year after The Homestead received its first skiers, the resort town of Gatlinburg, Tenn., the gateway to the Great Smoky Mountain National Park, opened up the area that is now known as Ober Gatlinburg. In 1961, Cataloochee began operations in North Carolina, starting that state on its way to the forefront of the Southern ski industry. (The state now boasts 10 areas, including several that are well known to Southern skiers, such as Beech Mountain, Appalachian Ski Mountain, Sapphire Valley, and Ski Hawksnest.)

To the north, in West Virginia's rugged Allegheny Mountains, ski areas sprouted up at such a rate that the industry has now become a major component in the region's economy. With their relatively high elevations and (by Southern standards) far-north location, West Virginia's mountains get a good deal of natural snow.

The first to see the potential of these mountains was Dr. Tom Brigham, a North Carolina dentist and developer of several ski areas in his home state. In the early 1970s, Brigham began work on what is now Snowshoe, created out of a natural bowl on Shaver's Fork in Pocahontas County. After a few disastrous snow years and enough financial problems to challenge the mind of a Rockefeller, the area has emerged as the South's premier ski resort. It has already spurred several other large developments in the vicinity.

Virginia, too, has mountainous areas, and lists five ski areas, including some—like The Homestead, Wintergreen and Bryce Resort—that are year-round vacation spots. Other Southern ski states include Missouri and Kentucky, with one resort each, and skiing can even be found as far south as Alabama and northern Georgia, also with one resort each. Florida still doesn't have a ski resort, but with the rapid pace of development of Southern ski areas and the new advances in artificial snow, it wouldn't be too surprising if the Sunshine State someday was hosting skiers.

The South's largest ski area and a major destination resort, Snowshoe has developed rapidly in the last 10 years. Located in the Allegheny Mountains of Pocahontas County, W.Va., it has a respectable 1,471-foot vertical serviced by seven lifts and featuring 37 runs. In the past few years, a new resort, Silver Creek, has been developed adjacent to Snowshoe.

Snowshoe Resort

In 1975 a major resort, Wintergreen, was developed in the Blue Ridge Mountains of Virginia. The 10,600-acre resort is private, and features year-round recreation in addition to the only vertical drop in Virginia that is over 1,000 feet.

Wintergreen Resort

SOUTHERN SKI AREAS

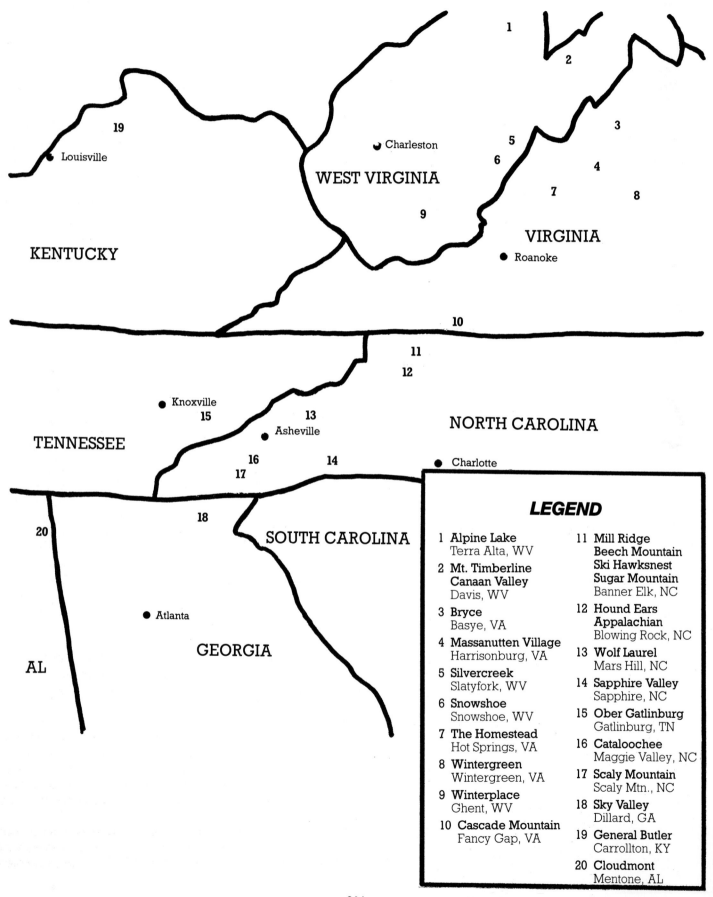

1
2

19

3

5

6 4

7 8

• Charleston

WEST VIRGINIA

VIRGINIA

• Louisville

KENTUCKY

9

• Roanoke

10

11

12

• Knoxville

15

13

NORTH CAROLINA

• Asheville

TENNESSEE

16

17

14

• Charlotte

20

18

SOUTH CAROLINA

• Atlanta

GEORGIA

AL

LEGEND

1 **Alpine Lake**
Terra Alta, WV

2 **Mt. Timberline
Canaan Valley**
Davis, WV

3 **Bryce**
Basye, VA

4 **Massanutten Village**
Harrisonburg, VA

5 **Silvercreek**
Slatyfork, WV

6 **Snowshoe**
Snowshoe, WV

7 **The Homestead**
Hot Springs, VA

8 **Wintergreen**
Wintergreen, VA

9 **Winterplace**
Ghent, WV

10 **Cascade Mountain**
Fancy Gap, VA

11 **Mill Ridge
Beech Mountain
Ski Hawksnest
Sugar Mountain**
Banner Elk, NC

12 **Hound Ears
Appalachian**
Blowing Rock, NC

13 **Wolf Laurel**
Mars Hill, NC

14 **Sapphire Valley**
Sapphire, NC

15 **Ober Gatlinburg**
Gatlinburg, TN

16 **Cataloochee**
Maggie Valley, NC

17 **Scaly Mountain**
Scaly Mtn., NC

18 **Sky Valley**
Dillard, GA

19 **General Butler**
Carrollton, KY

20 **Cloudmont**
Mentone, AL

CHAPTER SIXTEEN

DESTINATIONS

A SKI-AREA SAMPLER

The decades following World War II brought a surge in the construction of ski areas. After the war, Americans increasingly turned to the outdoors for their recreation, a trend that was given momentum by returning veterans such as the men of the 10th Mountain Division. At the same time, the nation was enjoying unprecedented economic prosperity, and Americans were finding more time—and more money—to pursue their favorite sports.

The mountains of both East and West echoed with the whine of chainsaws and the roar of bulldozers. In addition to well-known resorts such as Aspen and Squaw Valley, scores of lesser-known ski areas sprang up, including many in the flatlands of the Midwest.

Initially, much of the activity took place in the Northeast and the Far West. In more recent decades, however, Colorado became the site for many new destination resorts; by 1980 the state had surpassed both California and Vermont in its number of skier visits. Utah also has seen a recent boom in ski area construction, and Utah's Snowbird has taken a place among the nation's finest mountains.

For many years, new ski resorts tended to be constructed bit by bit, with new lifts, trails and hotels added as the money came in. By the 1960s, however, entire ski communities were being built from the ground up in a surprisingly short time. Sun Valley was a precursor to this trend; Vail, which opened in the early 1960s and is now a good-sized community, is one of its most notable examples.

In the last few decades, skiing has become a significant industry, worth millions and millions annually, and it has attracted the attention of America's major corporations. Aspen, for instance, is now owned by 20th Century-Fox, while Sun Valley was purchased by Earl Holding of the Little America chain of hotels. As American ski resorts grew, and as mountains became better groomed and added snow-making equipment, the price of lift tickets, lodging, food, and real estate increased in kind. Skiing took on a more businesslike flavor, and the ski bum, a breed that proliferated during the 1960s, became an endangered species.

The big boom in ski area construction slowed greatly in the 1970s. Environmental groups hampered or killed proposals for a number of new ski areas, including Mineral King, a California ski resort proposed by the Disney Corp. which was challenged in 1969. Since then, it has become increasingly difficult to build a ski area on public forest land.

In the last 10 years, many downhill skiers have literally turned their backs on ski resorts. They have taken to the woods on cross-country and touring skis, finding solitude and untracked snow away from the lift lines and moguled slopes. Some of them have simply given up Alpine skiing (often due to the expense) in favor of the more peaceful charms of cross-country. Others, however, practice what's been called "cross-country downhill"—skiing into the backcountry and making downhill runs using Nordic touring skis. Sondre Norheim's old turn—the telemark—has undergone a surprisingly strong renaissance, and the desire to practice it has lured some of these off-trail skiers back to the lift-serviced slopes.

But this and other types of off-trail downhill skiing (such as that done with the aid of a helicopter) are popular among only a small minority of the nation's skiers—American ski resorts are still going strong. There are over 700 of them, ranging from world-class destination resorts to small day areas. They are located from Maine to Alabama to Alaska—even in tropical Hawaii, where those willing to climb on foot can ski the snowfields of 13,680-foot Mauna Loa. What follows is a small sampling of the nearly endless variety of American ski resorts.

Outrun of a jump at Steamboat Springs, a major winter sports resort in northwestern Colorado. Its winter-sports history began in the early 1900s when Norwegian champion jumper Carl Howelsen, along with others, developed it as a center of ski jumping. In the past four decades many Olympic-caliber Alpine racers have received their training at Steamboat. The ski area now boasts a gondola and 11 chairlifts.   DPL

New York Gov. Averell Harriman, developer of Sun Valley and promoter of Lake Placid, cuts the ribbon at the opening ceremonies of Greek Peak, near Cortland, N.Y., on Jan. 10, 1958. Greek Peak now has four chairs and three T-bars.
Greek Peak

Seven Springs Resort, in southwestern Pennsylvania, as it appeared in 1946. Founded by Adolph Dupre, Seven Springs was one of the East's early ski areas, opening in 1937. With seven chairlifts, it is now the largest ski area in the state. Pennsylvania offers 38 other ski areas, most of them concentrated in the eastern part of the state and in the Poconos.
Author's collection

Vermont's Killington Peak is served by the longest ski lift in North America. The gondola rises 3,000 feet in three and one-half miles and serves trails up to 10 miles in length. One of the largest resorts in the East, Killington is only one of the areas that make Vermont a skier's mecca. Other major resorts include Bolton Valley, Bromley, Jay Peak, Mount Snow, Okemo, Pico, Stowe, Stratton Mountain, and Sugarbush Valley. Vermont also has dozens of smaller areas.
Killington Photo/Bob Perry

Skiers on the Pinkham Notch practice slope, White Mountains National Forest, 1936.   USFS

Ski instructor Louis Hechenberger with three students on Snow's Mountain, 1950. A rope tow and later a T-bar went up the hill to the right. Mt. Tecumseh is in the background. Skiing started in the area in the early 1930s and the CCC cut a trail on Mt. Tecumseh in 1937. In 1965 Olympic racer Tom Corcoran developed the mountain above Waterville Valley, N.H., into one of the finest ski areas in the East and an internationally known racing hill.

Mrs. Grace Bean, Waterville Valley   Louis W. Baker photo

Sugarbush Valley, near Warren, Vt., is another of the East's major ski areas. It possesses a vertical drop of 2,400 feet, 45 miles of trails, and eight chairs.

Sugarbush Valley

Skiing near La Crosse, Wis., 1940s.
State Historical Society of Wisconsin

Boyne Mountain, late 1940s. This resort in northern Michigan has a vertical drop of only 575 feet, but it is now one of the busiest ski areas in the country. It was started by Everett Kircher, who formerly owned several automobile and trailer agencies. Over the years, Boyne has hired some big-name skiers, such as Stein Eriksen and Othmar Schneider, to run its ski school. Kircher's company also owns The Big Sky Resort in Montana, initially developed by newscaster Chet Huntley.

Michigan State Archives

Early skiing in the Stowe, Vt., area. The Stowe complex consists of two mountains, Mount Mansfield and Spruce Peak, and is one of the nation's best-known ski areas as well as one of the earliest. Stowe was developed in the 1930s through the efforts of three men: Roland Palmedo, a New York investment banker; Sepp Ruschp, who arrived from Austria as a ski instructor and is now president and general manager of the Mt. Mansfield Co.; and C.V. Starr, a well-known insurance company executive. The Civilian Conservation Corps under the direction of Perry Merrill cut many of the first ski runs.

Author's collection

Although its vertical drop is only 370 feet, the Telemark Ski Area near Cable, Wis., gets a lot of mileage out of its ski hill. Telemark is one of Wisconsin's larger areas and is the site of a huge cross-country ski race, the annual American Birkebeiner. Tony Wise opened the resort in 1947, installed the world's largest snow-making system in 1961, and built Telemark's first chairlift in 1964.

Telemark

The magnificent peaks of the Tetons form a backdrop for skiers at Grand Targee resort near Alta, Wyo. Targee's top elevation of 10,200 feet ensures snow through most of the summer. This rather remote area also receives plenty of powder.   Grand Targee Resort

Steve Bradley, one of the West's pioneering ski-area developers, designed this "Bradley Packer," the prototype of today's snow-grooming equipment. This photo was taken years ago at Bradley's Winter Park Ski Area in Colorado.
Grand County Historical Society

Located way up in the northwestern corner of Montana, The Big Mountain is one of the most popular family areas in the West and is a major destination area for Canadians. The area opened in 1947. In the days before a chairlift served the top of the mountain, skiers could make the ascent on the "Big Mountain Sno-Cat."

Big Mountain

Bridger Bowl, a popular area near Bozeman, Mont., has been operated for years by the local ski club, which maintains very inexpensive rates. This photo was taken in 1961; the area is now served by four chairlifts. USFS

The old Brighton Hotel, built in 1894 at what decades later would be the site of Brighton Ski Area, located in Big Cottonwood Canyon 25 miles from Salt Lake City. The ski area was developed in the 1930s using WPA and CCC labor, while the hotel was torn down in 1946. Brighton is one of a number of ski resorts in the area, with Salt Lake City as the hub. They include Alta, Park City, Park City West, Snowbird, Deer Valley, Solitude, and Sundance. Brighton

The slopes of Ski Broadmoor, near Colorado Springs, Colo. The area is owned by The Broadmoor, the world-famous hotel, and caters both to hotel guests and local residents, offering a vertical drop of 600 feet. In the past few decades, Colorado has become a very big state for skiing. Its areas include A-Basin, Berthoud Pass, Breckenridge, Copper Mountain, Crested Butte, Keystone, Loveland, Purgatory, Vail, Beaver Creek, and Winter Park in addition to the four areas around Aspen —Aspen Mountain, Aspen Highlands, Buttermilk Mountain and Snowmass.   Broadmoor

Taos, a European-style resort in the mountains of New Mexico. It was founded by Ernie Blake, a Swiss ski instructor, and today is the largest area in the state, although it is not as well-known as some of its larger neighbors to the north in Colorado. New Mexico has only 11 ski areas but offers some very fine skiing despite its image as a desert state.

New Mexico State Records
Center and Archives

New Mexico's Hyde Park, a small day-use area that was built by the CCC in the 1930s. The Civilian Conservation Corps, a Depression-era, make-work agency that was established in 1933, helped construct ski areas throughout the United States.   NA

Ski Party at Hoodoo Ski Bowl, 1939. Located near the summit of Santiam Pass, Hoodoo was the first ski area in the central part of Oregon's Cascade Mountains. Its first rope tow opened in 1938 and in 1948 it installed one of the first double chairlifts in North America. It now has three chairs and two surface tows.   Hoodoo Ski Bowl

Stevens Pass has been a popular ski area for many years. Along with White Pass and Snoqualmie Pass, it offers Washington skiers ready access from major highways. This photo was taken in 1955; Stevens Pass now boasts seven chairlifts that serve 1,800 feet of vertical drop.   USFS

Vista House at the top of Mount Spokane Ski Area, 1952. It was built in 1934 as a fire lookout.
          Riblet Tramway Co.

Snoqualmie Summit Ski Area, 50 miles east of Seattle, Wash., in 1937. The CCC cleared a ski run here in 1933, and the area was operated by the Seattle Parks Department. Webb Moffatt, the present owner of three of the four ski areas at the summit, arrived in 1937. Today, the three areas—Snoqualmie Summit, Ski Acres, and Alpental—flank Interstate 90. Every year, thousands of children, many of them from nearby Seattle, take lessons from the ski school here, one of the largest programs in the nation.

Ski Lifts Inc.

Aerial view of Snoqualmie Summit (right), and Ski Acres (left), probably late 1940s.　　　USFS

Mount Baker's first chairlift, the Panorama Dome, was built by Riblet and opened in 1954.

Riblet Tramway Co.

Mount Baker Lodge, at Heather Meadows in extreme northern Washington. It was built in 1927 and was used by skiers until it burned down in 1931. Mount Baker's first rope tow was built in 1938. With consistently good snow lasting into late spring, the area has become very popular over the years.

Mt. Baker Recreation Co.

Mammoth Mountain in central California deserves its name. Twenty-three chairs and two gondolas serve this huge mountain, which sports a vertical drop of 3,400 feet. Dave McCoy, the area's founder, set up a portable rope tow in 1937 and by 1955 had installed a chairlift. Mammoth's season sometimes lasts into July, giving the hard-core skier eight months on the snow.   USFS and Mammoth Mountain

Snow King Mountain, just above Jackson, Wyo., with the beautiful Teton Mountains in the background. Twelve miles away lies the Jackson Hole Ski Area with Teton Village at its base. It has the largest vertical drop in the nation—4,139 feet. It takes only 12 minutes for the 63-passenger tram to make the 2.4-mile trip from the base to the top of Jackson Hole's Rendezvous Mountain.   DPL

The Mount Bachelor Ski Area near Bend, Ore. Famous for its late-season snow, the area was established in 1958 when members of Bend's Skyliners Ski Club set out to find a nearby mountain with an adequate snowfall. They found the right place—Mount Bachelor gets over 17 feet of snow per year. Oregon offers 15 ski areas, most of them concentrated in the western Cascade Mountains or the eastern Blue Mountains. Mount Bachelor

These people probably are still waiting to get on. A 1946 liftline at Mount Waterman, in the Angeles National Forest north of Los Angeles.

USFS

One of the oldest unaltered ski lodges in the nation is in daily use at Lookout Pass Ski Area, located just off Interstate 90 on the Idaho-Montana border.

One of the nation's most famous ski lodges is the massive Timberline Lodge, located on the south side of Mount Hood, east of Portland, Ore. The lodge was built in 1936-37 by the Works Progress Administration to provide jobs during the Depression. Its majestic and unique works of art have since placed it on the National Register of Historic Places. Timberline's patrons have a choice of three nearby ski areas—Mount Hood Meadows, Multorpor Ski Bowl, and the Timberline ski area. The lodge is one of the earliest large-scale ski hostelries, built just after Idaho's Sun Valley. Timberline's first chairlift, built in 1939, was the second in the nation and the first to use steel towers.

Timberline

Winter scene.
Oregon State
Library

No lack of snow
at the Timberline
Lodge.
Oregon State
Library

Interior view
showing the
lodge's massive
fireplace.
Oregon State
Library

Alaska's premier ski resort is Alyeska, 40 miles east of Anchorage at Girdwood. The base of this ski area is only 300 feet above sea level, but it rises to an elevation of 3,000 feet. Its first chairlift and a day lodge were constructed in 1960. Today, it offers five chairlifts, a large hotel, restaurants, lounges, and a large real-estate development. It caters both to Alaskans and to world travelers, as Anchorage is a stopover on international air routes. Alyeska Resort

A 1944 photo of the Douglas Ski Bowl, on Douglas Island opposite Alaska's capital city of Juneau, which can be seen across the channel. Douglas was not served by roads; skiers had to walk in to the area's rope tows. Juneau is now served by Eaglecrest ski area, just a few miles from downtown. USFS

North America's western-most ski area is located on Adak Island in Alaska's Aleutian Chain. Its short rope tow, however, has not operated in several years. Its ski "lodge" is a converted World War II Quonset hut, a relic from when the island was a base for 90,000 soldiers.

CHAPTER SEVENTEEN

POTPOURRI

UNUSUAL SKI PHOTOS

In hot, dry desert areas, sand can substitute for snow, with not entirely negative results. Above is a sand skier in Southern California, 1940. Below, sand skiers at the Great Sand Dunes National Park in southern Colorado, 1930.

Top: WASM
Bottom: CSM

Sand skiing in New Mexico.

Alaska natives were taught the craft of ski making, 1940.

Summer skiing on Mount Hood, Ore., late 1930s.

Summer sports at Paradise Valley,
Mount Rainier National Park,
Wash.   Author's collection

Summer sun at a California ski area, late 1940s.   FH

An Easter party at California's Sugar Bowl, late 1940s.   FH

A stray elk on a Colorado slope, 1920s. The elk looks like it could use a pair of skis as well.   DPL

Horse skiing at a 1917 winter carnival in Minnesota. This type of skiing, sometimes called skijoring, was popular in the early years of this century, perhaps due to the lack of lifts and availability of horses.   Minnesota Historical Society

One hopes this gentleman also had access to a pair of ski poles. Sugar Bowl, late 1940s.
FH

Testimonials to a warm spring day, Sugar Bowl, late 1940s. Technique and equipment may change, but this is one aspect of skiing that has remained the same.   FH

The shelter hut at Moon Valley, Minneapolis, Minn., 1946. This area had a 100-foot vertical drop. FH

Strangers to snow. South African mining engineers, touring mines at Wallace, Idaho, gave the sport a try, 1930s.   DPL

A 1920-style ski outing by women at Bemidji State College, Bemidji, Minn. Note the elaborate outfits and the predominance of knickers.   Minnesota Historical Society

Skiers of the Auburn Ski Club honoring something or someone at Cisco, Calif., 1930s.   WASM

A snowplow won't do much good to get down from
this spot.   FH

Waiting for a ride after a day's skiing, 1935.
                          Vermont Historical Society

One of the most unusual and colorful characters in the history of American skiing (and there have been many) is Carl Messelt, shown here with one of his inventions, an early day hang glider.

A Norwegian by birth, Messelt at age 20 came to the United States in 1923 to see what it was like. He was already an accomplished skier and had learned to fly, and he ended up being one of America's first ski instructors, teaching at the Pocono Mountains in Pennsylvania during the 1920s. A musician as well as skier and flier, he spent his summers barnstorming stunt planes and touring the East with his 12-piece band, The Vikings. He eventually worked on Wall Street.

Messelt was instrumental in promoting America's first indoor ski meet, held in New York's Madison Square Garden in 1936, and was appointed to both the American and Norwegian National Olympic committees. Due to his sometimes outspoken nature, he was subsequently removed from both committees. Now in his 80s and a widower (his wife was a member of the Du Pont family), Messelt lives in Los Angeles and is still very outspoken in his views on skiing, the management of the U.S. ski team, and life in general.

The hang glider, by the way, flew quite well, although once Messelt crashed it into some trees, and in another attempt, a friend of Messelt's crashed when the rope broke as the glider was being towed behind a car.

Carl Messelt

Allen's Antique Shop in Woodstock, Vt., apparently supplemented its income in the wintertime. Skiing boomed in the Woodstock area with the installation of several rope tows in the late 1930s. This photo was taken in 1940 by Marion Post Wolcott for the Farm Security Administration.

LC

SKIING'S LEGACY

SKI MUSEUMS

Statue of Snowshoe Thompson, the most famous of the early day California skiers, at the Western America SkiSport Museum, Boreal Ridge Ski Area, Calif.

The history of skiing is portrayed in a number of museums throughout the United States.

Ishpeming, Mich., the cradle of organized American skiing, is the home of the USSA's National Ski Hall of Fame and Museum. It houses exhibits that relate the history of the sport from the ancient Scandinavians through the present day, and its collection of historical skis is especially comprehensive. The Hall of Fame, located on the second floor of the museum, features pictures and biographies of skiers who have made significant contributions to the sport. Each year, several more are added to the roster.

Other museums are devoted to the history of skiing in a particular region. These include the Western America SkiSport Museum at Boreal Ridge Ski Area (Donner Summit), Calif.; the Colorado Ski Museum and Hall of Fame at Vail; and the New England Ski Museum at Franconia, N.H. (Cannon Mountain Ski Area).

In addition, at Littleton, Colo., one can find a fantastic array of privately owned ski artifacts at the Cafe Kandahar, which is owned by well-known skier Steve Knowleton. Winter sports equipment also is on exhibit at some of the general-interest museums that are located in the snowbelt states.

COLORADO SKI MUSEUM SKI HALL OF FAME

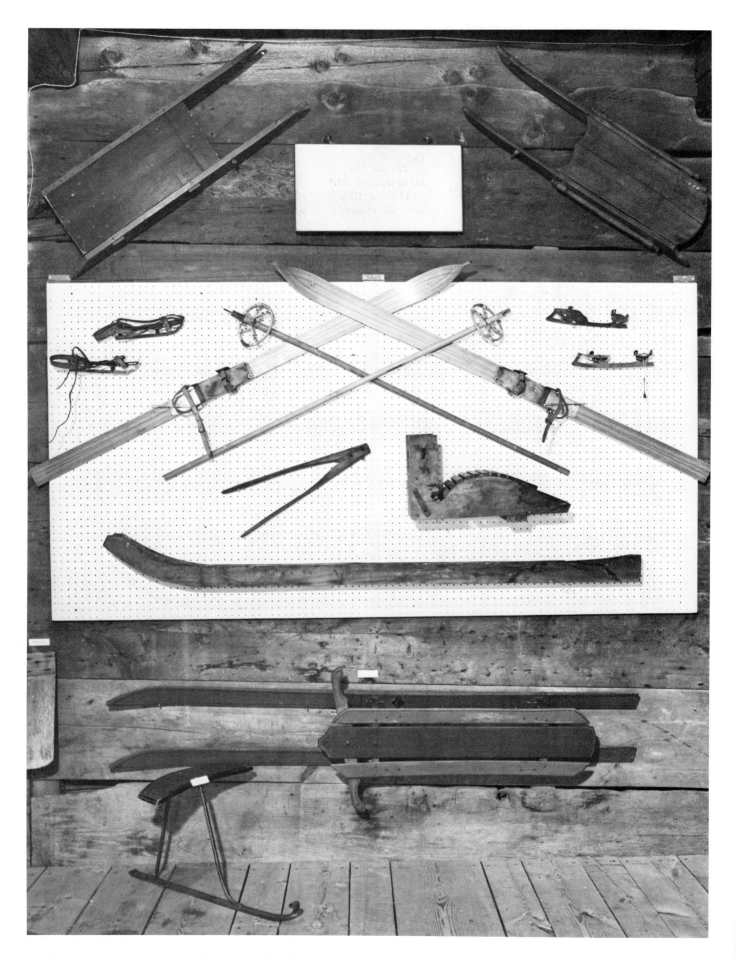

Winter-sports display at the Woodstock Historical Society Museum, Woodstock, Vt.

Woodstock Historical Society

The New England Ski Museum, located in a renovated maintenance building at the base of Cannon Mountain, Franconia, N.H. Started in 1982 by a group of area skiers, it is the nation's newest ski museum. Its media center is a memorial to Lowell Thomas, whose son, Lowell Thomas, Jr., contributed to the museum. The original Cannon Mountain tram, the nation's first ski tram, serves as part of the entrance to the building.

NESM

Colorado Ski Museum and Hall of Fame, located at Vail, was established in 1976 as a Colorado Centennial-Bicentennial project.
CSM by David Lockey

Interior of the Colorado Ski Museum.   CSM

Western America SkiSport Museum, a project of the Auburn Ski Club, is located at the Boreal Ridge Ski Area near Soda Springs, Calif. It was established to preserve the history of skiing in the High Sierras and the state of California.   WASM

Interior views of the Western America SkiSport Museum.   WASM

National Ski Hall of Fame and Museum in Ishpeming, Mich., where the National Ski Association was founded in the early 1900s. Started in 1954, it is the official museum and hall of fame of the United States Ski Association.

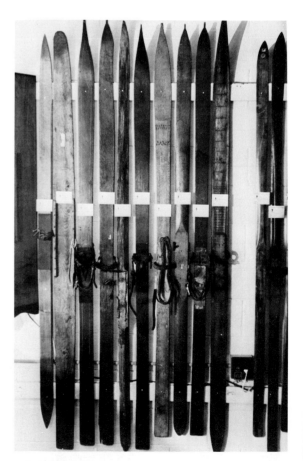

Equipment displays at the USSA's museum in Ishpeming.

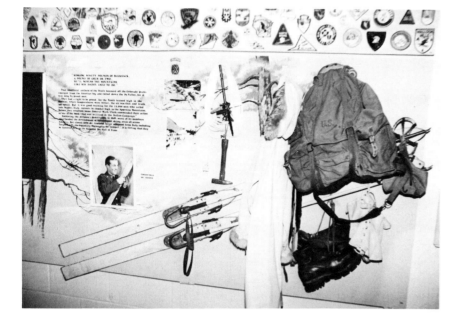

Interior views of the National Ski Hall of Fame and Museum.

The Hall of Fame is located on the second floor of the Ishpeming museum.

SELECTED BIBLIOGRAPHY

Abraham, Horst, *Skiing Right,* Johnson Books, Boulder, Colo., 1983.

Bays, Ted, *Nine Thousand Years of Skis: Norwegian Wood to French Plastic,* Mather Monograph Series #1, National Ski Hall of Fame Press, Ishpeming, Mich., 1980.

Bean, Grace H., *The Town at the End of the Road: A History of Waterville Valley,* Phoenix Publishing, Canaan, N.H., 1983.

Berry, I. William, *The Great North American Ski Book,* Charles Scribner's Sons, New York, 1982.

Besser, Gretchen R., *The National Ski Patrol: Samaritans of the Snow,* The Countryman Press, Woodstock, Vt., 1983.

Bowen, Ezra, *The Book of American Skiing,* J.B. Lippincott Co., Philadelphia, Pa., 1963.

Dole, Minot, *Adventures in Skiing,* Franklin Watts Inc., New York, 1965.

Enzel, Robert G. and John R. Urciolo, *The White Book of U.S. Ski Areas,* Inter-ski Services Inc., Washington, D.C., 1977.

Goodrich, Nathaniel L. (editor), *American Ski Annual,* Stephen Daye Press, Brattleboro, Vt., 1937.

Hagerman, Robert L., *Mansfield: The Story of Vermont's Loftiest Mountain,* Phoenix Publishing, Canaan, N.H., 1975.

Hovelsen, Leif, *The Flying Norseman,* Mather Monograph Series #2, National Ski Hall of Fame Press, Ishpeming, Mich., 1983.

Jay, John, *Ski Down the Years,* Award House, Universal Publishing & Distributing Corp., New York, 1966.

Kelner, Alexis, *Skiing in Utah,* Salt Lake City, Utah, 1980.

Magnaghi, Russell M., *Seventy-five Years of Skiing: 1904-1979,* National Ski Hall of Fame Press, Ishpeming, Mich., 1979.

Major, James and Olle Larsson, *World Cup Ski Technique,* Poudre Publishing Co., Park City, Utah, 1979.

National Ski Patrol System, *Ski Patroller's Manual,* revised eleventh edition, Denver, Colo., 1982.

Oppenheimer, Doug and Jim Poore, *Sun Valley: A Biography,* Beatty Books, Boise, Idaho, 1976.

O'Rear, John and Frankie, *The Aspen Story,* A.S. Barnes and Co. Inc., So. Brunswick, N.J., 1966.

Scharff, Robert (editor), *SKI Magazine's Encyclopedia of Skiing,* Harper and Row, New York, 1970.

Thompson, George A. and Fraser Buck, *Treasure Mountain Home: Park City Revisited,* Dream Garden Press, Salt Lake City, Utah, 1981.

Tobin, John C., *The Fall Line: A Skier's Journal,* Meredith Press, New York, 1969.

Various other editions of the *American Ski Annual* dating from the 1930s to the 1950s, in addition to old ski guidebooks and instruction manuals, newspaper clippings and magazine articles, as well as biographies provided by the National Ski Hall of Fame.

Bill Berry is perhaps America's leading ski historian. In 1928, he moved to Reno, Nev., from the East and became ski correspondent for many Eastern and international publications in addition to writing for the NEVADA STATE JOURNAL and the SACRAMENTO BEE. In 1963, he was named the first winner of the prestigious Harold Hirsch Award, given to the nation's outstanding ski writer. In 1966, he was named winner of the Julius Blegen Award, the highest accolade presented by the United States Ski Association. Berry has been a charter member of the Reno Ski Club (1929), a member of the Auburn Ski Club, and a charter member of the Far West Ski Association (1933). He was instrumental in founding the Western America SkiSport Museum at Boreal Ridge Ski Area, and from 1966 to 1972 he served as chairman of the National Ski Hall of Fame committee. He has skied since 1910, and he participated in jumping competitions until 1936. A much younger William Banks Berry is pictured at left.   WASM

The author with Snowshoe Thompson's original skis and mailbag, Western America SkiSport Museum, 1984.

ABOUT THE AUTHOR

Stan Cohen, the author of *A Pictorial History of Downhill Skiing,* spent 11 years in the ski business during the 1960s and early 1970s, running a ski shop, a ski school, and co-managing a ski area in Missoula, Montana. In 1976, he established Pictorial Histories Publishing Co. and has since written or published over 50 books. A native of West Virginia, he holds a degree in geology from West Virginia University and now lives in Missoula with his wife and two children. When not writing and publishing history books, he enjoy skiing, traveling, and collecting antique Americana and automotive items.